32
Persian
30
GATOS DE RAZA
AF815364
Cheetah
AUSTRALIA
PARAGUAY
Gs.3.
TANZANIA
70/.
Acinonyx jubatus
CHINA
20
SHARJAH
Animal Rescue
adopt a shelter pet
44
USA
2010
Le chartreux
RF
USAirmail
45
AMERICA
ITALIA
600
DEVON REX
Gatos Asiáticos
Hong Kong '97
Burmés
15
correos 1997
Cuba
$2 USA
NIPPON
82
5-PTG
9 SEP
1999
NIPPON
EGYPT
1980

lonely planet

WHERE *to* CHEAT *on* YOUR CAT

THE CAT LOVER'S TRAVEL GUIDE

DIANA HELMUTH
with Eliza Washington

For my partner in travel, Joanna Robinson,
and the world's friendliest cat, Bug.

Contents

CAT-TOPIAS 133

BIG CATS: SANCTUARIES 171

BIG CATS: PUBLIC PARKS 199

Foreword

THERE IS SOMETHING ancient in the relationship between cats and cities. Long before they were pets, cats were presences — watching from rooftops, slipping between market stalls, and claiming the warm patches of stone the sun had touched. They did not belong to anyone, yet they belonged completely to the place.

Walk through Thissio in Athens on any afternoon, and you will find them: stretched across marble steps, tucked into the shade of an olive tree, or watching the foot traffic on Apostolou Pavlou with an air of supreme indifference. Athens has always been a city of cats. They are woven into its texture, its light, and its particular quality of stillness. To notice the cats of a city is to notice something essential about it — its rhythms, its warmth, and the generosity with which it extends itself to the small and the stray.

When we opened our cat café in Thissio and began filling our space with cats waiting for a home, we didn't anticipate the response from cat lovers visiting from far and wide. Travelers come to Athens from every corner of the world. They climb the Acropolis, they sit in tavernas, they watch the light change over the Saronic Gulf. And then they find their way to us. From Latin America, from Australia, from New Zealand — people who have crossed hemispheres to be here, and who carve out an hour, sometimes on multiple occasions during their stay, just to sit among our cats. They arrive as tourists. They leave as something else. A little softer, perhaps. A little more themselves. But Athens is just one place. People travel far and wide to see the world— and we know no matter what, there are people who need to see a cat (or two or three).

We have watched people from countries that share no common language connect with each other entirely through a cat — laughing together as a tabby climbs from one lap to the other, even exchanging phone numbers so they can compare notes on which cats they loved best. Cats, it turns out, are one of the few universal languages. They erase distance. They make strangers into companions. And sometimes they do something more.

There was a cat who lived with us for nearly six months. Gentle, patient, a little overlooked — as some cats are. She had not found her person. Then a man came from Denmark, sat down at a table, and before he had even ordered his coffee, she was in his arms. She stayed there for the rest of that visit. She was in his arms the next day, and the day after that. On his last morning in Athens, he could not leave her behind. He adopted her, carried her home across a continent, and she has been with him ever since.

We think of that story often. A cat who waited, a man who traveled thousands of miles without knowing why, and a city that held the space for them to find each other.

That is what cats do. That is what places, at their best, do too.

- **DIMITRIS SGOUROS,** Cat Cafe Athens

Introduction

I HAVE A CONFESSION. I am not a cat lady. I am an anxious cat lady. I love to travel, but I hate to leave my cats behind. I'm often consumed by guilt at the thought of them in the care of a stranger, feeling confused as to why I have abandoned them, and lamenting that I cannot simply lean down and explain, "I'll be back soon, mommy just needs 96 hours away from home with her Slack turned off."

What is the solution to the anguishing guilt of being separated from my cats? Cheating . . . *with other cats.*

In the following pages, we have assembled a travel guide showcasing locations across the world where you can meet warm-bellied felines snoozing in world-class hotels, gape at Africa's "big three" cats pawing through their home savannas, or sip tea on a mountain terrace with a farm kitten on your lap. You don't have to own these cats. You don't have to clean their litter boxes or bandage your hands after trying to convince them to wear a leash. You can simply do what you're supposed to do with any cat, anywhere: bask in their

glory. Many of these locations are supported by non-profit groups, or even just a cadre of well-meaning neighbors. We provide instructions for how you can even help, too.

Cats are present on every continent in the world (except Antarctica, but they're working on getting an indoor at McMurdo). They are instinctually tidy, independent creatures whose self-sufficiency is so profound that it'll hurt your feelings. They are the ancient wardens of libraries and craft houses – fighting pests off ancient books and precious textiles. They are the modern sidekick for the renter who cannot afford a backyard, or whose landlord prohibits the claws and barks of the larger version of "man's best friend." Sure, they won't bite a burglar, and they don't pay rent. But we care for them as if our legacy depended on it. A cat doesn't just show up loving you. You have to earn it.

The biggest downside of cats is that they are territorial. They do not like new places. There are exceptions of course: a whiskered face peering out of a pop star's bubble backpack, or a furry-eared explorer on a leash, romping through National Forests. But our shock at these exceptions proves the rule: cats don't like to travel.

That's why, if you're gonna cheat, you can't bring them home. You have to go to their place.

If you already know why cats are good for you, the value of these cat-traveling experiences don't need to be explained. And if you don't know yet, I'm so excited for you to find out.

We promise we won't tell your cat at home.

Note to Readers

You got this book (or someone gave you this book) because you love cats. We have the utmost respect for that love. That's why we wrote this book with the ethics to support it.

It's an unfortunate fact that many private zoos, roadside attractions, hotels and even plain old rich people take their love for cats to an exploitative level, prioritizing human delight over the health and comfort of the cats in their care.

You will not find places like that in this book.

Does that mean the locations we have collected here are less exciting than a bedazzled private zoo where you can pet a baby tiger? Maybe. Does it also mean you don't have to worry about what happened to that baby tiger's mother, and feel like you committed an animal rights violation? Definitely.

All the cafes, parks, teahouses, bookstores, sanctuaries, rehabilitation centers and public squares profiled in this book were selected with care by a slightly obsessive woman in her mid-30s who is potentially capable of taking a human life if anyone ever so much as looks wrong at her fur babies. "Would I be happy if my own cat wound up here?" she asked herself. If the answer was no, we didn't include it.

The cat cafes we profile never de-claw, overcrowd, or pressure their cats to interact with humans. All the big cat sanctuaries are registered with the Global Federation of Animal Sanctuaries (GFAS) and/or Big Cat Sanctuary Alliance (BCSA). Their focus is on the rehabilitation of formerly harmed animals and forbid petting, drugging or forced separation between parent and cub. Many of the parks and rescue centers profiled in these pages are staffed by volunteers and run on tight budgets. The majority of ticket sales go directly back to the cats, and if there are no tickets, we always suggest ways to donate so you can get a warm, fuzzy feeling knowing you helped make the world a better place for warm, fuzzy creatures.

We hope you enjoy meeting these cats on the best of terms: *theirs.*

CITY CATS

PARIS, FRANCE

Paris

FRANCE IS KNOWN TO have one of the highest cat populations in Europe – even boasting its own rare breed (the Chartreux, a demure shorthair with “blue” fur, orange eyes, and the world’s most petite meow). France’s capital city, like almost everything else it does, takes its love of felines to a haute level. Amid the luxe couture window displays, the legions of crepe stands and bistros, the striking monuments and graffiti, Paris’s most iconic residents can be seen slinking down chic cobblestone alleys, napping on sunny balconies, or simply sitting on an open windowsill, watching the world go by with inspirational levels of ennui.

Parisians have made their love for their aloof, effortlessly elegant residents no secret, with renowned artists like Théophile Steinlen, Suzanne Valadon and Pierre-Auguste Renoir having regularly featured feline muses in their work.

As the celebrated poet Jean Cocteau said, “I love cats because I enjoy my home; and little by little, they become its visible soul.”

So, whether you’re visiting Paris to watch the catwalk at fashion week, to attend Europe’s largest cat show at the annual ExpoZoo exhibition, or just to see the original Le Chat Noir poster at Musée Carnavalet, keep your eyes open for the soul of the city: its feline dwellers.

Cimetière de Montmartre

LOCATION
20 ave Rachel,
18ème, Paris.

SPECIAL NOTES
The cemetery is generally open until 6pm, and is closed on Saturdays. Volunteer caretakers request that you do not feed the cats.

Lush greenery and bustling foot traffic line the sunny, cobblestone streets of Montmartre, the historic neighborhood that gave birth to the Moulin Rouge, the cancan, and the original Le Chat Noir nightclub. This is a perfect place to take in classic Parisian architecture as you make your way through a chorus line of stunning 19th-century stone and brick buildings, vibrantly decorated with colored plaster and adorned with wrought iron balconies. Montmartre benefits from being less crowded than other Parisian neighborhoods, but still features a number of iconic bistros, cafes, and even the occasional taco stand.

Less than a mile from the Musée de Montmartre is Cimetière de Montmartre, home of *la mort bohème*, the final resting place of some of France's most beloved celebrities, and dozens of (living) cats. This spot is a great choice if you need a break from the crowds.

No one knows how the cats first got here. But in 1978 local photographer Michel Cambazard set up a rescue group, L'École du Chat, which began to offer them healthcare, vaccinations and regular food. About 50 cats currently call the Montmartre cemetery home – a controlled population, thanks to the continuing work of Cambazard's organization.

The cats here can be shy and elusive, and it's recommended that visitors walk quietly through the graveyard to have the best chance at spotting them pattering among the memorial statues or sunning themselves on a warm gravestone.

Parc de Bagatelle

Have you ever wanted to feel like Marie Antoinette, lounging in a public park worthy of Versailles, nibbling on cakes and gazing at cats? What better place than the botanical gardens of Parc de Bagatelle? The resident pleasure pavilion, the Château de Bagatelle, was constructed in 1777 on a bet between Marie and the Count of Artois that he couldn't build it within three months. She lost the bet but gained a castle: a gilded manse that the royals named *Bagatelle* – the French term for "little nothing." The precisely manicured gardens that surround the trifling chateau are home to over 10,000 roses, as well as waterfalls, bridges, grottos, water mirrors, ducks, peacocks and about 50 cats.

While the birds are more brazen, it's best to visit the park on a quiet day if you want to hold court with the cats. The four-legged royals of Bagatelle are tended by a dedicated group known as La Féline du Chlojolie. In addition to feeding, sheltering, spaying and neutering their furry regents, they also facilitate about 30 adoptions a year through their veterinarian program.

For a nice day trip, go to Boulangerie Zest on 1 rue Ernest Deloison and grab a coffee, a classic baguette sandwich and a pastry. Then take a 10-minute stroll to the park entrance and pick your favorite spot amongst the regal gardens to prepare for a cat sighting.

LOCATION

Bois de Boulogne, rte de Sèvres à Neuilly, 16ème, Paris

The Parc de Bagatelle bus stop is right across the street.

SPECIAL NOTES

Open daily until about 5pm in winter and 8pm in summer. This park is part of the grand Bois de Boulogne, a public trove of lakes, trails and botanical gardens.

"Paris's most *iconic residents* can be seen slinking down chic cobblestone alleys, napping on *sunny balconies*, or simply sitting on an *open windowsill*, watching the world go by with inspirational levels of *ennui*."

A stray *chat noir* sizes up your panache as you approach her local haunt.

Le Café des Chats

LOCATION
9 rue Sedaine, 11ème, Paris.

SPECIAL NOTES
The cafe is open Tues-Sun from noon to 9:30pm. Menu prices range from €6 appetizers to €30 for a two-person cheese plate.

Located in the Marais, Le Café des Chats is a cozy, peaceful sanctuary near the heart of one of the trendiest arrondissements in the city. On the rue Sedaine, a short eight-minute walk from the Maison de Victor Hugo, more than a dozen cats lazily roam a cafe reminiscent of *Friends*' Central Perk with a dash of Diagon Alley from Harry Potter, while their human servants handle all the work in the kitchen. Whether they were born on the street or suddenly found themselves without a home, each cat has been carefully selected for their sociable personality and strong potential as a cafe cat. Because of the meticulously curated vibes (and health and safety standards), outside cats are not permitted, but children of all ages are welcome, as long as they are supervised by an adult.

While you may be tempted to take one home as your own personal food critic, these feline gourmets have been permanently adopted by the cafe owners. However, you can join them for an artisanal, homestyle meal six days a week. It's open late – a great place to grab an espresso and get some fuzzy cuddles in before the Bastille's vibrant bar scene heats up.

Le Café des C

CITY CATS

VENICE, ITALY

Venice

HAVE YOU EVER WANTED to feel like otherworldly fae royalty, floating lackadaisically down the thoroughfares of an enchanted sunken city as your retinue ferries you to an important meeting with ambassadors from the feline court?

Venice has you covered.

Venice is a medieval city that, in defiance of logic, physics and common sense, has a lagoon as a foundation and canals for streets. Cats and Venice have been besties since plague rats hit the port city during the Middle Ages. The beleaguered citizens put the furry fighters in charge of their homes until the problem cleared up. What began as a marriage of convenience turned into an eternal love affair, helping Italy claim its position as a top country for cat lovers.

Not only does the Italian government have legal protections for cats and cat colonies, but Venice also has a spay/neuter program that relocates strays to established colonies on the islands surrounding Venice, where organizations like Dingo Venezia provide food, care, shelter and protection. In fact, cat colonies are not allowed to be moved without first consulting a veterinary service and getting the express permission of the mayor.

Libreria Acqua Alta

LOCATION
C. Longa Santa Maria Formosa 5176b, Venezia.

SPECIAL NOTES
Open seven days a week. Not wheelchair accessible. This is a popular tourist spot; to avoid crowds, try to visit right at opening or closing.

You'll know you've found this literary cat haven when you turn a corner and see a fig tree at the end of a stone courtyard, books spilling out from beneath its boughs. There are several entrances to Acqua Alta, but this one is considered the front.

The secondhand bookshop was founded by Luigi Frizzo after he grew tired of selling books out of his gondola. To protect the books from Venice's regular high tides (the aforementioned *aqua alta*), Frizzo has forgone traditional bookcases, instead shelving them in gondolas, bathtubs and canoes. From books that have experienced too many high tides to be readable, entire walls and stairs have been constructed. The shop doesn't just house books – it is made of them.

Almost as soon as Frizzo opened his bookstore in the early 2000s, a pregnant cat waltzed in. Frizzo named her Tigre, and she became a permanent fixture near the cash register. Now, after some adoptions and the arrival of additional orphans, about five felines can be found prowling the dark, page-packed lanes of the shop – chasing away rats and posing for photos. Most are quite happy to accept a tribute of affection from tourists (Mussipull, in particular, is known for his tireless purr).

FIRE EXIT
ACQUA

Torcello

If you're feeling overwhelmed by the mobbed Venetian tourist scene but still need more cats in your life, Torcello is at your service.

Hop on the ferry, which whisks you across the Venetian Lagoon, stops at a few colorful ports, and finally docks at the sleepy, green isle of Torcello.

Initially populated by those fleeing the likes of Attila the Hun and largely abandoned over time, the island's human population has dwindled to a meager 15 souls. The cats, however, are everywhere: curled up in grassy fields, strutting down the herringbone brick walkways that line the canals, sunning themselves on the stone carvings outside the Museo di Torcello, or enjoying a meal served by the few remaining Homo sapiens.

Because of its legacy as one of the oldest inhabited parts of the Venetian Islands, Torcello is home to the oldest church in Venice and a prime example of Byzantine art and architecture: the Basilica di Santa Maria Assunta. If you like to pair modern art (and lagoon walks and flamingo sightings) with your cat vacation, check out the Casa Museo Andrich.

LOCATION

The public *vaporetto* departs from Fondamente Nove in north Venice, and transfers you to a new boat on Burano island.

SPECIAL NOTES

The *vaporetto* runs just about 24 hours, with 1-2 departures per hour. Tickets are €9.50 (valid for 75 minutes, essentially a one-way ticket) or €25 (valid for 24 hours).

"Cat colonies are not allowed to be moved without first consulting a *veterinary service* and getting the express *permission of the mayor*."

A Venetian community cat makes his rounds on the parapets over the canals.

Forte Marghera

LOCATION
It's a 20-minute tram ride from Piazzale Roma in Venice to Forte Marghera, or you can drive.

SPECIAL NOTES
See the island's events calendar at fondazionefortemarghera.it. There's lots of free parking, and it's mostly wheelchair friendly.

Walking through quaint, ancient European cities can feel like walking through a dream. At Forte Marghera – the 19th-century military fort turned outdoor museum, cultural center and cat sanctuary – that dream is less of a romance, and more like an acid trip (albeit, a good one).

Picture yourself crossing a bridge, walking toward a red brick gate engulfed in trees. You emerge from the walls into what you expect will be a small village, but instead it's a military base made of white stucco and red tile. Out of the corner of your eye, you catch an orange tail disappearing behind a well-trimmed hedge. You look behind the hedge: a clown is reciting poetry to a small audience. Returning to the main path, you let the flow of the crowd carry you past a series of cat houses to a tall circus tent. It's another day at the Circo al Forte, just one of the events hosted at Forte Marghera.

You might return on a sunny day to enjoy a barbecue and see a car show, then come again another time for a zombie-themed escape room. The point, it seems, is variety and whimsy; you can never quite be sure what you will get. With the exception of reliable cat sightings.

This Venetian island is also home to Europe's largest cat colony. You won't have to work hard to see them – they'll probably walk up to greet you. The cats are unusually friendly and content thanks in large part to I Mici del Forte, a vanguard of volunteers who provide the cats with food, comfy houses and veterinary care. Consider donating them a few euros to support their efforts.

CITY CATS

PITTSBURGH, PENNSYLVANIA, USA

Pittsburgh

IF YOU'VE EVER SPENT a sunny afternoon strolling down the sidewalks of one of the ketchup capital's many neighborhoods, you've probably noticed an inviting, amiable atmosphere that lingers over cozy porch hangouts, historic churches and open-air cafes. It's nothing less than you'd expect from the original site of *Mister Rogers' Neighborhood*.

Whether they're inspecting the growth of new plants in spring or hunting lightning bugs floating through the summer evenings, feline "yinzers" (as Pittsburgh residents affectionately call themselves) can be spotted just about everywhere. In winter, you can catch them peering through Pittsburgh's iconic stained-glass windows, watching rabbits hop across frozen brick lanes.

Even famous Pittsburgher Andy Warhol wasn't immune to their charm – he eventually adopted 25 cats, 24 of whom he named Sam. Be sure to check out pieces of his *25 Cats Name Sam and One Blue Pussy* book at the Andy Warhol Museum in the North Shore neighborhood.

Black Cat Market

LOCATION
5135 Penn Ave, Pittsburgh.

SPECIAL NOTES
LGBTQ+ friendly and women owned. For weekend visits and/or for larger parties, the staff recommends making a reservation for a cat room. Their schedule can be found at blackcatmarketpgh.com.

The three c's at the Black Cat Market are cats, coffee and community. The staff here are dedicated to homes for needy cats, coffee for thirsty humans, and community growth. They provide space for pet therapy sessions, are a drop-off and pickup location for Livy's Library (an organization that provides free books for children), and offer a meeting space for the PA Unemployment Council. Since opening in 2018, they have connected over 1200 homeless cats with happy homes. It's fair to say that the owners of the Black Cat Market are experts in mammalian connection.

If you're looking for more than a casual coffee date with the Burgh's favorite felines, you can attend one of Black Cat Market's regular ongoing events such as their book club or paint nights, or even rent the whole space for a private event.

If you're planning to be in town for longer than a few days, consider joining their rewards program (one free cat room visit for every $45 spent), along with frequent visitor passes. They also offer student discounts – including "Study Hall" bookings. If you're homesick for the sight of your cat all curled up on your desk as you cram for exams, there's likely a kitty here who would be happy to substitute.

HE BLACK CAT MARKE

Kitty Queen Cat Rescue

Practice your downward dog next to an outstretched cat, or sink into Savasana while a puffball purrs on your chest. Kitty Queen's gentle flow Kitty Yoga class is open to all levels of humans, graciously led by one of the teachers from The Lotus People.

And as a bonus, the cats prancing under your bridge pose are adoptable. Kitty Queen is a multiroom cat cafe and event space that also functions as a no-kill shelter, ensuring all cats have been spayed or neutered, microchipped, tested for FIV/FELV and vaccinated.

Their popular yoga classes are designed for beginners, and are welcome to anyone over the age of eight. But if you feel that stretching is best left to cat limbs rather than your own, check out some of Kitty Queen's other cat-focused events, which range from paint parties to ice cream socials. The multiroom rescue center has a lot going on and can also be rented for private events.

Kitty Queen is officially a nonprofit, relying on donations of money, cat supplies, foster care, and generous humans willing to spend time socializing with young kittens – which has to be the greatest way we can think of to help fulfill the eightfold path's mandate for charity and compassion.

LOCATION

4552 McKnight Rd Suite 400, Pittsburgh.

SPECIAL NOTES

Admission to the Cat Lounge is $5 per person. Special events are also consistently affordable. Check out kittyqueencatrescue.com for the latest schedule for the Cat Lounge and the yoga classes.

"Whether they're *inspecting the growth* of new plants in spring or *hunting lightning bugs* floating through the summer evenings, feline "*yinzers*" (as Pittsburgh residents affectionately call themselves) can be spotted *just about everywhere*."

A royal feline finds the sunny spot at Kitty Queen, Pittsburgh

The Prison Cats

LOCATION
3001 Beaver Ave, Pittsburgh.

SPECIAL NOTES
Technically this place never closes, but the best time to see the cats is early morning or around dusk. You can buy extraordinarily cool Prison Cats merch on their website, too: pghprisoncats.org.

The Western State Penitentiary may have been abandoned by humans in 2017, but the cat colony – living here since 1826 – did not get (or care to read) that memo. This makes it one of the oldest continuing cat colonies in the country.

The so-called "prison cats" got their first known caretaker in the 1970s, a man by the name of John "Porky" Sapovchak. He was followed by Nancy Barylak, who pioneered TNR (trap, neuter, return) programs for the massive colony, which had ballooned to a population of around 400. Nancy was succeeded by Tara Czekaj, Melissa Rubin and Lilian Akin, along with several neighbors, and today the prison cat population has been reduced by over 90%, to about 25 cats. This makes the Pittsburgh Prison Cats one of the most successful TNR programs in the US. However, cats from other parts of Pittsburgh occasionally move in, making the work somewhat never-ending. One imagines word on the cat street travels fast, for places that serve up a good meal and and a free de-worming.

The lead volunteers are supported by various veterinary charities, Amazon wish lists and a GoFundMe. However, annual expenses can run up to $14,000 to properly take care of every cat that comes through here, and much of that has come from the volunteers' own pockets. It's a nice idea to donate some food or funds. We imagine Mr. Rogers would smile to see it.

CITY CATS

ISTANBUL, TÜRKIYE

Istanbul

IF THERE WAS EVER a city bidding for the title of "most cat-friendly in the world," the crown would almost certainly go to Istanbul.

The term "stray cat" loses all meaning once you get to the Bosphorus. Istanbulite cats are viewed and treated not as feral vermin, but as something more akin to communal pets. Cats are tucked into every possible open space you can imagine: loafing calmly on subway turnstiles, snoozing on out-of-stock makeup shelves at the drugstore, or peering at you from the top corner of your hostel's shower (presumably, having just eaten a spider). Their soft, slow-blinking comfort around people, even large crowds, is a testament to how well they are treated.

Estimates on how many cats live in Istanbul range from 30,000 to as many as one million. Their good treatment comes partially from the prevailing religion, Islam, in which cats are considered inherently clean and blessed. However, it's a specifically Turkish saying that warns, "If you kill a cat, you must build a mosque to be forgiven by God."

If it takes a village to raise a child, it takes the City of Cats to demonstrate that stray cats can be practically indiscernible from cats with human households. Istanbul shows that while all feral cats are strays, not all stray cats have to be feral.

Fenerbahçe Parkı

LOCATION
The park is on the Anatolian side of the city; follow Fener Kalamiş Cd. to the end, toward the water. Several city buses stop nearby, or you can drive.

SPECIAL NOTES
Keep your eyes peeled for a hedgehog sighting!

Do you feel the deep-seated desire to roll yourself in a pile of catnip and be mobbed by as many cats as possible?

That's not, technically, a service offered at Fenerbahçe Parkı, but it is probably something you can get away with.

Located on the southern coast of Istanbul in the Kadıköy district, Fenerbahçe Parkı is the perfect spot to have a quiet outdoor lunch, unwind after shopping on Bağdat Caddesi, or simply enjoy the company of loads of cosmopolitan cats. The name "Fenerbahçe" means "Lighthouse Garden," and during the Ottoman Empire, it was the site of a prominent lighthouse. Over the years, the need for the lighthouse diminished, and the park evolved into a green space, welcoming hundreds of cat guardians. Go for a jog alongside piles of snoozing cats. Watch children and felines share a playground. There is even a dedicated yoga and meditation area, if you'd like to host your own impromptu cat yoga while listening to the lapping waves of the Sea of Marmara.

In addition to the regular amenities like easy access to public transportation, public restrooms, benches and picnic tables, there are a couple of cafes with stunning views of the sea. Keep a few treats in your pocket, and it won't be long before a few cats decide to join your outdoor table.

Hagia Sophia

There are many reasons to visit Hagia Sophia Grand Mosque – too many to list here. Even setting aside its rich history dating back to the 6th century, its status as a symbol of the nation of Türkiye, and its permanent place in the pantheon of human innovation, physically experiencing the Hagia Sophia is breathtaking. The marble decor could have you staring at the walls for hours, let alone the art.

And here, residing in this wonder of the world, there are cats. And I do mean "reside" quite literally. They have their own small houses, tucked into the sacred walls.

The most famous was probably Gli (2004-2020), who lived in the mosque during peak internet cat obsession. However, cats have lived in the Hagia Sophia long before social media. In Islam, cats are considered ritually pure and are welcome to move freely in religious spaces. The Hagia Sophia is currently home to a white, long-haired cat who appears to be taking over Gli's duties as an official mascot, sometimes spotted sitting on the ledge of the minbar next to the imam during Friday service.

The care of the mosque cats is usually undertaken by museum staff, who ensure they have regular meals, healthcare, and a clean litterbox. Mosque cats across Istanbul, especially here, are often some of the friendliest and cleanest you will meet.

LOCATION

Sultan Ahmet Ayasofya Meydanı No:1, Istanbul.

SPECIAL NOTES

Modest dress (including women's hair covering) is required for entry. Parts of the mosque close to the general public during prayer times. Check the schedule online before heading over.

"If there was ever a *city bidding* for the title of '*most cat-friendly in the world,*' the *crown* would almost certainly go to Istanbul."

A curious cat, and some humans, too, checking out the Hagia Sophia Grand Mosque in Istanbul.

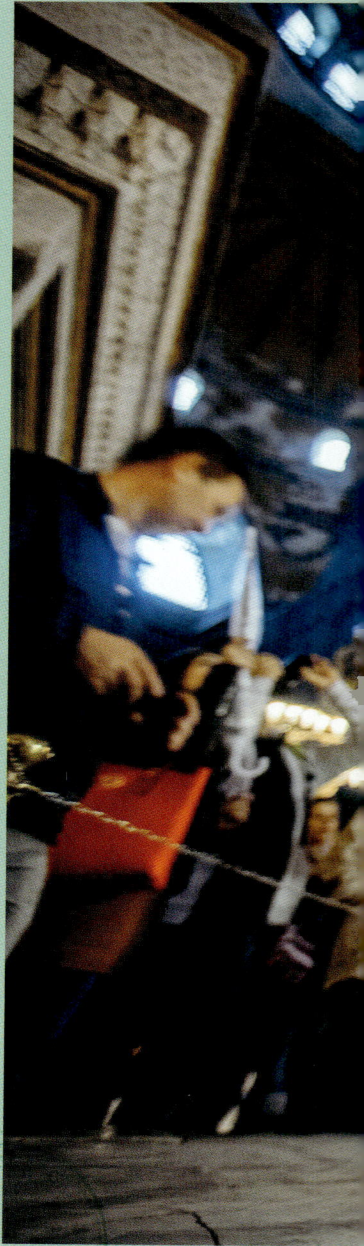

Istiklal Caddesi

LOCATION
The M2 metro, T2 tram, B1 train and several buses all stop along Istiklal.

SPECIAL NOTES
This is a particularly vibrant (read: loud) neighborhood, 24 hours a day. If you crave peace and quiet, book a hotel a bit further out from Istiklal.

Have you ever wanted to combine the shopping of the Champs-Élysées, the cable cars of San Francisco and the feline density of your favorite cat cafe? Istiklal Caddesi awaits you. The .87-mile (1.4km) Taksim Meydanı in the north and ends at Tünel Meydanı in the south, and cats roam just about every inch of it, alongside the bustling humans. Historic architecture rubs shoulders with quirky vintage shops, noisy cafes swing you into the night, and glamorous morning patisseries greet you during the day. It's crowded, to be sure, but it's never dull.

While just about every neighborhood in Istanbul has a healthy number of cats, Istiklal Caddesi is particularly popular. The avenue's large cat population is sometimes attributed to its proximity to one of Istanbul's most iconic fish markets, Balık Pazarı. Located at the corner of Istiklal and Sahne, fishmongers have been advertising anchovies and marketing mackerel here since the Ottoman Empire, and the aromas are like a homing beacon for the neighborhood's community cats. They can often be caught waiting for a stray sardine to fall or weaving between the ankles of the fishmongers.

CITY CATS

TOKYO, JAPAN

Tokyo

JAPAN'S TITANIC CAPITAL BLENDS sleek glimpses of the future with a reverence for traditions, and its love for felines seems to braid the whole timeline together. Tokyo is overflowing with cat cafes, cat islands, and cat cosplay (especially on Harajuku's Cat Street). This is the birthplace of global cat icons the likes of Hello Kitty, Bananya, Pokemon's Meowth, and Sailor Moon's Luna.

The *maneki-neko* (or "beckoning cat," the little white cat statue that waves you hello and goodbye) can be found in just about every storefront and entryway across the city. According to one legend, the cat became a symbol of good luck after a young man opened up a shop and suffered from slow business – until a cat came along and began to wave at passersby. The owner tried to shoo the cat away, but it wouldn't budge. Eventually, people would stop on the street to say hello to the cat, and then, enter the shop. Business boomed, and the man realized the cat was his lucky charm. The original *maneki-neko* statue can be viewed at the 17th-century Gotokuji temple – a working spiritual center. Leaving your own statue here is said to bring you fortune. Visit today, and a tsunami of hopeful, waving paws will greet you hello.

It is not an understatement to say if you love cats, and you're coming to Tokyo – welcome home.

Temari no Oshiro

LOCATION

Kichijoji Petit Mura, 2-33-2 Kichijoji-Honcho, Musashino-shi, Tokyo.

SPECIAL NOTES

There is no time limit on your visit, and for a bit extra, you can even feed the cats yourself. Check out current hours at temarinooshiro.com

Tokyo may not have invented the cat cafe, but its arguably where the concept has been perfected. Crowning a single one the best among the whole city is certainly impossible. However, if you only have time to visit one cat cafe, many would agree it should be this place.

It's estimated that a staggering 60+ are active just within the city limits, and each has its own unique spin, including rare breeds, rescue cats, or dramatic, anime-inspired palaces. The latter is the case at Temari no Oshiro.

The front door is located inside the shopping "village" of Kichijoji Petit Mura, whose facade is built out of plump, cartoon trees and an awning of bubblegum pastel tiles. Stepping inside Temari no Oshiro is like stepping straight into a forest scene from a Studio Ghibli-inspired book of fairytales. About 20 cats live here in the cafe, hopping between giant mushroom pads, hiding in trees, or chasing each other through round huts. The cafe serves up fare to match the décor: pudding parfaits garnished with cat-shaped cookies, mochi corn dogs, and drinks like strawberry milk chai, white peach tea and marshmallow cocoa (although they will serve you a basic coffee and some fries, if you ask nicely.).

イット村
T MURA

綾小路きみまろさん
来店
2016
七福神めぐり
ご朱印帖
ご予約販売中
¥2,500
お土産は「TAMARU」で。
国産
ガーゼ手拭

Yanaka

Many cities have cat cafes, and some even have a cat-filled public park. Tokyo has Yanaka – an entire neighborhood that is more or less dedicated to cats. Most live on the street, but calling them feral would be a gross mischaracterization, considering how tenderly and communally the human residents of Yanaka look after their four-footed neighbors.

Yanaka's *shotengai* (main street) is Ginza, which also serves as a bit of an architectural time capsule of pre-war Tokyo. The street is packed with modest little shops tucked under wooden balconies and awnings flanked with paper lanterns, every edge bedecked with waving paws and smiling whiskers. Highlights include the cat-tail-striped donuts at Shippoya, or the *taiyaki* from Maneki-ya, where the traditionally fish-shaped waffle dessert comes in the shape of (what else?) a *maneki-neko*. You can even order a custom statue in the colors of your own cat back at home over at Yanakado gift shop.

If you want to hang with the real cool cats, however, head for the headstones. Yanaka Reien is a sprawling graveyard complex shaded by thick green leaves and packed with overgrown bushes that occasionally meow. This is where most of Yanaka's cats can be found during the day, sunning themselves or nibbling on snacks left by their doting neighbors. People frequently stop by to provide healthcare, grooming, and general TLC, and cats often recognize and run to greet their favorite humans.

However, one of the best places for the truly cat-obsessed in Yanaka is Nenneko-ya. It's a departure from the wham-pow glam of Tokyo's premier cat

LOCATION

Yanaka neighborhood is in northeast Tokyo, near Nippori station.

SPECIAL NOTES

Most shops and restaurants are open from about 11am-7pm.

cafes, but the humble little building is far more than first meets the eye. Dip down in the entryway, and you'll find yourself among a happy pile of snoozing cats, but also a wall-to-wall museum of cat paraphernalia that the owner, Mie Kuba, has been collecting for more than 25 years.

The most interesting part of the place, however, is probably the shrine in the back. Kuba claims she never planned to build a shrine seriously dedicated to cats. The memorabilia she had collected began to spill out of the museum, and when she started using the area around the old torii gate outside to store what she couldn't fit inside, people began leaving offerings of flowers and cat food, along with images of their recently deceased pet cats. Eventually, Kuba realized what was going on, and took it upon herself to hang the pictures, gradually building the space into a thoughtful, proper spiritual shrine. Today, she welcomes any visitor who seeks a moment of prayer and connection for a departed cat.

A ginger cat enjoys the outdoors in Yanaka.

"It is not an *understatement* to say if you *love cats*, and you're coming to Tokyo – *welcome home.*"

Tokyo doesn't have a feral cat problem. It has a community cat blessing.

My Cat Yugawara

LOCATION

244-1 Fukuura, Yugawara, Ashigarashimo District, 259-0311, Kanagawa. Manazuru is the closest station.

SPECIAL NOTES

The hotel also welcomes guests traveling with their own cats.

The title of this book is *Where to Cheat on Your Cat* as a bit of a joke. But there's one place in Japan where it's hardly a joke at all. You can literally check in at a hotel and sleep with another cat.

My Cat Yugawara is a traditional Japanese *ryokan* (hotel) located in Hakone, a resort town about two hours southwest of Tokyo. Guests sleep on tatami mats and futons, are provided with yukata robes, and can enjoy the soothing hot waters of the nearby Hakone onsens. But the real perk of staying here is your overnight roommate: a cat.

It's more than just a cheap thrill. For people thinking about cat adoption, owner Akihiro Ochi wanted to create an experience that went beyond the typical cat cafe – one that truly helps people test the reality of living with a cat for a few nights. Guests first come into the hotel for a trial run at the cat lounge, where cats and humans get to know each other (and staff observe them). Once a little trust has been built, the guest can request to effectively foster the kitty for their stay at the hotel – complete with feeding them treats and curling up for purring bedtime snuggles, but also, litterbox cleaning, ensuring proper behavior, and patiently enduring their furry roommate's 3am zoomies.

CITY CATS

TAIPEI, TAIWAN

Taipei

TAIWAN'S SOFT GREEN MOUNTAINS rub shoulders with neon-streaked skyscrapers. Its residents are a melting pot of Indigenous Pacific Islanders, Iberian traders, Japanese settlers, Chinese nobility and Dutch sailors. But everyone can probably agree who really runs this island: cats.

Cats pop out of parades, add flair to street fashion, and wander in and out of art exhibits. They often reside in temples, pampered as guardians and harbingers of good luck. Scattered across the island are human-grade hotels for cats, along with cat-themed hotels for humans. One of the most famous is Doris Home in Yuchi, about 135 miles south of Taipei, a modern, clean-lined B&B where the resident cats more or less pounce on you upon arrival.

Finding a cat cafe is easy – just walk into a normal cafe, and meet the cat who is already living there. However, for cafes that actually brand themsleves as such, the cats are not held in a seperate room, like you'll see in most North American setups. Instead, the kitties hang out while baristas whip up frothy espressos and fruity cream teas just on the other side of the counter. There's a level of trust and love here between cat and human that is rarely found anywhere else on Earth.

Houtong Cat Village

LOCATION

The train from Taipei takes about 50 minutes and costs about NT$47 (US$1.50), dropping you off downtown.

SPECIAL NOTES

Most shops are cash only. If you want to stay nearby, check out hotels in Ruifang or Jiufen, which have larger tourist infrastructure.

About an hour outside of Taipei, Houtong was once home to around 6000 coal miners and their families. When the mine closed in the 1990s, the humans left. The cats, who had been chasing pests that wandered into the village from the forest, remained – haunting the empty shops and quiet streets. In 2008, photographer Peggy Chien (aka "Cat Mother") began a project capturing the faces of these forgotten felines in the mountains north of Taipei. These images tugged at the heartstrings of a number of cat-besotted humans, and soon volunteers poured in to implement TNR, feeding and healthcare programs.

Now, Houtong has shifted its identity from coal town to cat town. This is because cats are everywhere, roaming free in what amounts to a post-industrial takeover. A small population of humans do live here, too, mostly to keep the feline-centric economy alive with feeding stations, vet clinics, de facto cat cafes (you simply can't keep them out) and souvenir shops. Wherever your eye falls, odds are a cat will cross your path. Many shops sell cat treats, which the community cats will happily eat right out of your hand.

Unlike most strays (or rather, residents), the Houtong cats are quite friendly, having grown up in front of cameras and receiving food from humans. Still, plenty of warning signs remind visitors that these are, after all, wild animals. It's best to take a seat on a bench and wait for a cat to approach you. It won't take long.

Kitten Coffee Garden

Welcome to the mother of all cat cafes, operating in Taipei since 1998 – and to which initially, nobody showed up.

It wasn't until a local TV station did a report on the new concept – and cat lovers of the world flocked en masse to its doorstep – that Kitten Coffee Garden became the feline hall-of-famer that it is.

The cafe's reputation often precedes it. It's clean and lovely, but in most respects, it's a standard-issue Taipei cafe. The notable exception being the menagerie of animals roaming around, which includes not only 12-20 cats, but two dogs, and one bird.

Tracy Zhang, a co-owner and co-founder, humbly states that Kitten Coffee Garden wasn't the first cafe in Taipei to have a cat – they were simply the first to have been "discovered."

Like most cat cafe setups in Taipei, the cats at Kitten Coffee Garden are not cordoned off in their own play area but are free to explore the entire place to their hearts' content, hopping on tables and napping on empty chairs. You can purchase snacks for the cats and even feed them by hand.

A common question from foreigners is, with all this intermingling, do the cats ever steal a sip of your drink? According to Zhang, the answer is no – the cats don't want your coffee. They do, however, have a thing for frosting. Watch your cake for paw marks.

LOCATION
129 Fuhua Rd, Shilin District, Taipei.

SPECIAL NOTES
This cafe has been written about by dozens of travel writers, under all three of its names. However, the address has always been the same, as has the purple and white sign.

"There's a level of *trust and love* here between *cat and human* that is rarely found anywhere else on *Earth*."

Street cats in Taipei lounge along the sidewalk, waiting for a stray treat or a friendly ear scritch.

Maokong

LOCATION
The gondola is part of the Taipei public transportation system, and departs from just behind Taipei Zoo.

SPECIAL NOTES
Many teahouses are open until 10pm on weekdays, even later on weekends. Monday is the normal closure day, except for Yao Yue, which is open 24 hours, 7 days a week. Tickets are NT$180 (US$5.50).

Does a better match exist than a purring cat and a warm cup of tea?

Outside Taipei Zoo, a gondola awaits to take you to this cat and tea heaven. The 20-minute ride lifts you up from the clamoring city into the silence of sky, while the rainforest canopy floats hundreds of feet below.

Up here, morning mist wreaths through forest branches, stepped terraces of tea farms descend the mountainsides, and the whole scene is punctuated by cat statues, cat posters, and cat-shaped treats in cafe windows. Officially, Maokong is not a cat village in the same way that, say, Houtong is. But it wouldn't be Taiwan if a mountain village wasn't at least *partially* inhabited by felines.

Maokong's main attraction is tea – especially Tieguanyin and Baozhong oolongs. Many Taipei city slickers hop the gondola just for a cup paired with a dreamy sunset over the forested mountains.

A cat is equally likely to wander past your table at one of the teahouses up here as it is to follow you into a nearby tea field tour. If you're still coming up short on your cat sightings, though, check out Cats Got Nothing to Do Café, roughly a half mile from where the gondola drops you off, to say hello to the regular cats. Farther away, set apart from the majority of shops, there is a blink-and-you'll-miss-it bookshop known by many English names, the easiest to remember probably being Elsewhere Café. Here, you can bury your nose in a fresh book, sample sweet pots de crème and thousand-layer cakes, fall into one of the fantastic art pieces on the wall, or sip a cup of oolong next to the resident shop cat.

CITY CATS

BEIJING, CHINA

Beijing

A LOT CAN BE said about China's capital city, but one fact worth mentioning is that leopard cats (solitary, nocturnal felines with distinctive black spots) live on the outskirts of town.

Although they look magical enough to outlive time itself, leopard cats only became the local apex predator after the regular leopard was pushed out in the 1990s. They are a reminder that if we want a world where humans can live near wild animals, we have to carefully consider their needs alongside our own.

Beijing is also home to the Cat Aficionado Association (CAA), the largest cat registry in China. It caters to pedigreed and non-pedigreed cats, but also exists to promote China's native breeds like the Li Hua Mao (aka the "Dragon Li"). Animal advocacy groups have been on the rise here for the past decade, and Beijing Adoption Day has seen over 2000 strays adopted out since its inception in 2011.

Cat cafes have been opening at a record pace across China; there are 12 in Beijing alone. Admittedly, feral cats have long been a problem in the dense and ancient city, but today, most Beijingers have a positive attitude toward their community cats.

The Forbidden City

LOCATION
4 Jingshan Front St, Dongcheng, Beijing.

SPECIAL NOTES
The Forbidden City is open most days except Mondays. Tickets must be purchased online ahead of time, and can sell out during the peak season, so book early.

As the walled heart of political power in China for over 500 years, the Forbidden City is as mysterious as it is massive. The 178-acre (72-hectare) complex is the home of China's largest and best-preserved collection of historic architecture, along with tides of gorgeous antiques, halls of transcendental art, and, of course, the most important feature of any human monument: cats.

Technically, the Forbidden City is the largest palace in the world, offering plenty of room for feline courtiers. Over 150 cats are said to live here (some estimates go as high as 300), many rumored to be descended from the pets of the Emperor himself. Today, the emperor is no more, the aristocracy has been ousted, but the cats live on – technically, they are the only full-time residents that remain in the Forbidden City. The palace's current human staff still have the high honor of ensuring their health and well-being. Compared to the average street cat in Beijing, these cats live a good life: they are well-fed, receive medical care, and are part of a healthy TNR program.

The Forbidden City is one of China's most iconic monuments (which is to say: it's hella busy). Since cats are creatures of superior taste and sensibility who often avoid crowded areas, those hoping to hold court with them should seek out quieter areas away from the center of the palace and avoid visiting on weekends or holidays.

The Great Wall – Mutianyu

The Great Wall is made up of multiple fortifications stretching over 13,000 miles (21,000km). Unlike its more popular sibling site, Badaling, Mutianyu is known to be less crowded, so there's more peace and quiet and fewer people competing for attention. This is especially helpful if you're angling to run into the (very seriously named) Mutianyu Great Wall Cat Guard.

This is the title for the diligent, dedicated community cats that have taken this section of the Great Wall as their charge. Chief Mu, for example, is the top guardian, a gray and white battleaxe of a cat who, it is rumored, has a powerful meow that puts all other squad members on alert. Commandant Yu, a tabby, is considered a master of public relations, and is tasked with distracting you from harming any antiquities via his adorableness (as claimed by the Mutianyu Great Wall website).

If you really want to get interrogated by all the kitty security guards, go in the off-season; winter is much slower, and the cats are much more likely to come out into the quiet in search of a snack.

LOCATION
Mutianyu Rd, Huairou District, Beijing.

SPECIAL NOTES
Mutianyu is about 1½-2 hours outside Beijing by car; the site is not accessible by train. Tickets start at ¥45 (about $6.28), and the last entry is at 5:30pm.

飲

"Cat cafes have been opening at a *record pace* across China."

A cat ensures your table will be warm for you in Beijing.

Gubei Water Town

LOCATION
About two buses per day depart from Dongzhimen station in Beijing.

SPECIAL NOTES
Regular day passes are ¥150 (about $20.91), but prices vary if you buy a tour package or stay in local accommodations. Gubei swells during holidays; go another day if you can.

Gubei feels like a picture-perfect movie set from a Kung Fu drama. But instead of hidden princesses and warrior monks, the stars here are cats.

Built in the 2010s, Gubei was designed for tourists to experience a taste of ancient Chinese life through immersive architecture and traditional crafts. It also quickly, and perhaps inadvertently, became a place that many cats call home. There is no official charity that manages the cats here, but the business owners have all silently taken on the role of caretakers, providing food, shelter and veterinary care. The love is evident: these cats are some of the healthiest and liveliest stray cats you'll meet around Beijing. And if you're telling me you don't want to sit by the water under the glow of Chinese lanterns and gaze at the lights of the Great Wall while you pet a cat named Michelle Yeoh, I won't believe you.

For the best chances of meeting a new feline friend, consider staying in local accommodations to take advantage of the cat-friendly calm of early mornings and evenings.

CITY CATS

ATHENS, GREECE

Athens

ZOE PORPHYROGENITA, EMPRESS OF BYZANTIUM in 1042, had a cat. His name was Mehlebe (sometimes written Mechlempae) and he had a vanguard of servants dedicated to his upkeep: spoon-feeding him from dishes of gold, attending to his shopping, and carrying him about in his favorite basket.

The cats of Athens seem to remember this example. They are all a version of Mehlebe. And we, the guileless public, are the servants. Greek tour guide Leonidas Argyros puts it well when he says, "Athens is full of cats, treating all passersby almost like slaves who simply exist and use their hands to serve them."

There are so many stray cats in Athens, it seems disingenuous to have a list describing where to go. You don't have to *go* anywhere. All you need to do is walk out your front door and open your eyes. Walking through Athens, you have the sensation that you are seeing through time. And this is because, more often than not, you are. Peer down one of the main roads from downtown, and your eyes will take in buildings built last year, last decade, last century, and long before the Bible was written. The cats are the time travelers, wandering from the doorways of falafel huts and disco bars, through the aisles of Hadrian's library, and up into the Hill of the Muses.

Their astronomical presence and general friendliness are a bit odd considering Greece's history. There were virtually no cats in classical Athens. An ancient Greek was more likely to have a lion on a leash than a cat in his living room. It took the influence of the Roman Empire, and perhaps figures like Empress Zoe, to import cats from their native Egypt and into Europe.

Today, cats can be seen across just about every part of Greece. If there is a historic site, a village or an island, odds are there are heaps of cats there. There are a handful of organized charities in Athens that do their best to ensure the many (many, many) street cats that live here get basic healthcare. However, most of the cats are taken care of by do-gooders in the community, without any particular affiliations.

A calico gets some shade from an ancient column in Athens.

VIA AERE
PAR AV

Acropolis

LOCATION
Plug "The Acropolis" into any map app, and you'll get directions.

SPECIAL NOTES
As of 2024, you must get a timed entry ticket to visit the Acropolis. Check their website for occasional free entry days.

Cats have apparently been living in the Acropolis longer than anyone can remember. You can catch them lounging casually in the Parthenon, sunning themselves before the columns at the Temple of Athena Nike, and chasing mice through the nooks of the Propylaea. Most of them are quite friendly; unlike with most strays, if you offer a friendly "pspsps," there's a decent chance the cat won't even flinch, but will slow blink back at you, ready to accept some pets or a spare treat.

Titan was a behemoth tom had his own pin on Google Maps of his latest whereabouts, complete with a 4.9-star rating. Some argued he was cooler than the ancient religious citadel itself. "The Acropolis? The Parthenon? Please," said one reviewer. "The first thing you ought to see is Titan." Titan was in fact so friendly, and thus fed so much, local rescue group SMART (Successfully Managing Animal Rights Today) took him into custody. He may be the only stray cat in history who had to be put on a diet for his own safety.

There is a broad community effort to care for the many cats who live here. They ensure the cats at the Acropolis (and across most parts of Athens) have a safe environment, receive some basic healthcare, and get a decent meal.

Kerameikos

Most of the cats in Athens' popular historic sites are happy to be in your face, inviting adoration from the sidewalk or the sunbaked stones of ancient archeological sites.

The cats at Kerameikos, however, reflect the energy of the cemetery itself: they are more subdued, underrated – black cat energy, if you will (regardless of actual fur color). People often overlook this place, and those that wind up here are just fine with that.

Kerameikos was once the coolest place to be buried in Athens. It was also the start of the Hierá Hodós, the sacred route where the cults of Demeter and Persephone would begin their procession during the ritual of the Eleusinian Mysteries. Some burials here go back to the Bronze Age. Today, it accepts almost no new burials, but exists as a pause from the busy swirl of tavernas and traffic in the rest of Athens. In spring, the space between the stones bursts with emerald green, and wildflowers wave over the sites of ancient death. A small museum catalogues the historic artifacts that just sort of turn up in such a place, the ground occasionally coughing up 1000-year-old treasures.

A cemetery mixed with an archaeological site is a cat's wonderland: quiet, full of sunny stones, and dotted with small pockets and tubes to duck into when they need a rest.

LOCATION

Ermou 148, Athens.

SPECIAL NOTES

The cemetery has different areas. The gated archaeological sites tend to be open from 8am-3pm in the winter, and 8am-8pm in the summer. You may also catch a few tortoises sunning themselves, in addition to the cats.

"The cats are the *time travelers*, wandering from the doorways of falafel huts and disco bars, through the aisles of Hadrian's library, the eaves of Zeus's temple, and up into the *Hill of the Muses*."

Three friends enjoy some magical sunset light in Kerameikos.

Cat Cafe Athens

LOCATION
Nileos 54, Athens.

SPECIAL NOTES
They are usually open from noon to 9pm. Reservations are strongly recommended (visit catcafe.gr to book), however, they do accommodate walk-ins on a first-come basis. Also, they have opened a franchise model. In case you want to start a cat cafe in Athens.

It seems almost ironic – verging on bizarre – for a cat cafe to exist in Athens, simply because there are usually more cats wandering around Athens than you can count. You could pull up a chair next to a patch of sunbathing felines with a cardamom coffee in one hand and a handful of treats in the other and simply call it a day.

However, there are good reasons to head to Cat Cafe Athens. The first being, well, the cats here are far more likely to be clean and disease-free than their scruffy street cousins. Also, a good portion of the money made here goes into caring for all of Athens' street cats. This was part of the motivation for Natalie and Dimitris Sgouros, who founded the cafe in 2023 – the first cat cafe in Greece. Initially they assumed they would only be popular with tourists and set up shop in an international district. To their happy surprise, most of their customers are locals. Since opening, they have facilitated the adoption of over 100 cats.

The shop offers a lovely atmosphere: a big, ocean-colored wall studded with cat-sized parapets and floating nap pods, under a roof of overlapping vine leaves. Ambient jazz floods the air. A hopeful piano sits in the corner.

There is a separate bedroom for the cats, in case they tire of the nonstop flow of attention and want a quiet room to rest. But for the most part, they are content to flit overhead, nap on one of the brightly colored cushions, and accept a pampering from you, their new, strange servant.

CITY CATS

NEW YORK, NEW YORK, USA

New York

BURIED INSIDE *THE NEW YORK TIMES* archives is a trove of cat stories, most taking place during the city's Gilded Age (around 1870 to the 1900s). According to *Times* journalist Andy Newman, this was apparently a golden era of feline exploits in New York. The stories range from the antics of pampered indoor-onlys to the heroics of ragtail strays. Many feature a cat popping in to interrupt a formal party or getting into a scrap with a lobster. But the point is their quantity, and what it evidences: New York has been in love with its cats for centuries.

Today, New York's love for its cats can be seen in neighborhood bodegas, where resident furballs have become so beloved (they even have their own Instagram, @bodegacatsofnewyork) they are in the process of being reclassified as working animals in order to slink past the law that prohibits an animal from existing near a deli counter.

The state of New York is home to about 16 cat cafes, nearly half of which are in the Big Apple itself. New York is, arguably, the most walkable city in the US, which is perhaps why Peggy Gavan founded New York's own walking tour dedicated to cat history. Cats About Town Tours will take you through the sites of some of New

York's most beloved cat-related moments, such as the former site of the Capitol Hotel, where Blackie lived as the resident mouser (and was a favorite drinking buddy of Teddy Roosevelt), or Borough Hall, where the blind cat, Jerry Fox, saved the building from a deadly fire. You can even bring your actual cat on the tour while admiring these other cats (New York is happy to help you blur the line between cheating on your cat and ethical non-catogomy). At Christmas, a squad of felines raids a neighborhood nativity scene in Brooklyn, batting the Christ child off his hay and loafing in his place, while the statues of Mary and Joseph look worshipfully on.

It would be denial to say forgotten strays are not a problem in a city this large. However, in response, every New York neighborhood seems to have a squad of dedicated Samaritans who take it upon themselves to set up TNR and healthcare programs for community cats, often at their own expense.

New York's beloved bodega cats always find the best spots to keep watch.

FLO

The NY Cat Film Festival™

LOCATION
The exact theater changes each year. Check their website for this year's details: catfilmfestival.com.

SPECIAL NOTES
Tickets run at a charitable $25, making it one of the most affordable things you can do in New York City.

For when internet cat videos aren't enough and you need a harder dose.
Officially, New York's Cat Film Festival is "an exploration through film of the fascinating felines who share our lives, creating a shared audience experience that inspires, educates and entertains." Unofficially, it's just a great way to spend an afternoon in a dark theater with a bunch of other cat-obsessed people.

The festival is held in October each year (typically around the 16th, to highlight National Feral Cat Day) at a rotating number of grand theaters across New York. The films are a series of shorts, ranging from the absurd, such as Casper Flatman's *Oh Catnada!*, a rumination on what an actual cat-led country would look like; to the profound, such as Tania Bashkatova's *Loki, Ukrainian Cat*, an actual documentary of a Ukrainian stray's journey from the fields of war to the hills of Ireland.

Tracie Hotchner founded the festival in 2017 as an encore act to The NY Dog Film Festival. Ticket sales are a feel-good purchase: part of every sale goes to a local nonprofit that cares for strays.

Fun fact: the NY Cat Film Festival does not always take place in New York. Past screenings have taken place in Colorado Springs, Prince Edward Island, and Washington, DC.

PRODUCER

Algonquin
Algonquin

The Algonquin Hotel

The Algonquin is not a mere hotel. It is a New York institution. Similarly, the Algonquin Cat is not so much a cat as a symbol of the New York dream: it doesn't matter if you were born in a ditch, one day something could happen that will catapult you to the top and crown you king of the city. Virtually every cat that has been granted the title of "The Algonquin Cat" began their life as a stray (the most recent was born in a feral colony on Long Island) before being whisked away and brought to live a life as fancy as any Manhattan child's: premium food, a private bedroom, daily brushing, birthday parties, and a fashion show in its honor.

The only rule is that the cat must submit to a name change. Every tom has been named Hamlet, and every queen, Matilda. (Hamlet was in honor of frequent guest John Barrymore's most famous role. No one knows where Matilda came from.) None of the cats have seemed to mind.

The Algonquin Cat may be New York's most famous cat. It has been featured in *New Yorker* cartoons, boasts an Instagram account of over 40,000 followers, and has been gifted at least four oil paintings.

Walk into the hotel today, and you might catch the current Hamlet making his rounds between the foyer couches, hopping across mahogany book-shelves, or taking a ride on a gleaming brass luggage dolly. Due to New York health code laws, he has a geofence collar that prohibits him from leaving the lobby (which is to say, no, unfortunately, Hamlet cannot stay in your room). But he does have a private area in the back, in case he needs a rest from public attention. Which doesn't seem to be too often.

LOCATION
59 W 44th St, New York.

SPECIAL NOTES
Reports claim that the current Hamlet is most social in the morning, or around 5pm. The Blue Bar, which is in the hotel's lobby and thus in Hamlet's domain, pours drinks until about 1:30am.

"New York has been *in love* with its cats for *centuries*."

A shop cat on duty.

The Cat Museum of New York City

LOCATION
Check the website for the latest event listing: catmuseumnyc.org.

SPECIAL NOTES
Tickets to events, hosted at hip venues throughout the city, often sell out. Grab yours in advance.

New York is famous for the magnitude and quality of its museums, so it seems only natural that it has one dedicated entirely to cats.

The Cat Museum of New York City's mission is to explore the historic, indelible connection between human and feline, chiefly through art. Their focus is on the cats who give a city its character: the feral, the unhoused, the community-loved, and those lucky enough to have New Yorkers as their guardians. The museum hosts events such as cat-themed art exhibitions and fundraising parties where feline-styled burlesque performers strut the stage, and makeup stations are at the ready to transform you into (who else?) your cat. They also put on family-friendly, outdoor coloring book sessions and drawing tutorials by famous cat artists like Heloísa Nora of *Poorly Drawn Cats*. The museum aims to raise awareness of the cat overpopulation crisis and support the efforts of those trying to solve it, including cat rescuers, shelters, veterinarians, fosters and individual heroes on the street.

The Cat Museum of NYC has been active since 2024, however, like most of the cats it serves, it has no home address, managing to do everything it does from a variety of donated spaces including bars, parks and other museums. Their website lists a calendar of events and also accepts donations to help them manifest a permanent, physical location.

The Cat Museum
of New York City
gatos

CITY CATS

CAIRO, EGYPT

Cairo

THE LOVE OF CATS is still alive and well in the place that gave the world its very first cat goddess. The ancient desert cemetery of Saqqara (a day trip away from Cairo) was found in 2018 to also be the home of a vast cat graveyard, where hundreds of mummified cats were laid to rest in the fifth dynasty. Walk inside the cool tomb walls, and you can see millennia-old paintings of striped tabbies sitting under chairs or pouncing on prey.

Modern Cairo is a dense city of between 10 and 20 million people (depending on the time of day) with 38 official neighborhoods sprawling outward from the warm artery of the Nile into the surrounding desert. And every single one of them has a huge population of cats.

A hard truth about Cairo is that, although the city is rich in pride and history, most humans who live here do so with very modest means. It's a testament to the indelible Egyptian love of cats, then, that even with limited resources, the street cats are as healthy and friendly as they are. Egypt's first official animal charity group was founded in 2001, and now there are more than seven, providing healthcare and TNR programs not just for street cats, but often dogs, horses and donkeys as well. But most of the care given to these cats is by everyday people, offering snacks, shelter, fresh water and a scratch behind the ears. This is just a part of daily life for most Cairenes.

The cats in Cairo, however, are muscular survivors. They eat trash and sleep in back alleys. But they also seem to remember that they are descended from a society that worshipped a god that had their face.

Wait in line at the local pita shop, sit in the dusty red glow of sunset puffing a shisha, walk down the shores of the inky Nile next to the shaabi-blasting felucca boats, and a cat will almost certainly cross your path. They are used to good treatment. Make an offer of kindness, and they will likely saunter over to say hello.

Cats have been living in and around Cairo for thousands of years.

Khan el-Khalili

LOCATION
Khan el-Khalili is more like a neighborhood, and the best starting spot is probably the medieval Bab Al-Ghuri gate, near the Mosque of Sayyidna Al Hussein.

SPECIAL NOTES
Most shops stay open until 11pm.

You know that obligatory outdoor market scene that accompanies any medieval film set in the Middle East? Well, if you're looking for a real-life version of that, Khan el-Khalili has you covered. Traders have been hawking their wares here since the 14th century. Almost everything is sold in this 12-acre (5-hectare) labyrinth, from plastic souvenirs and cheap papyrus drawings, to premium spices, haute perfume, gold jewelry, and hand-hammered metal lamps. It's the exact kind of place where you could follow a cat down a covered alleyway on a hot night and soon enough find yourself completely – and pleasantly – lost.

Many of the cats that live in Khan el-Khalili are shop mascots, believed to bring good luck (and keep the rats away). They're quite shameless – wandering in and out of eateries and cafes, snacking on your leftover shawarma, and meowing at you for attention.

If you are (somehow) having trouble spotting cats in this dreamy, *Arabian Nights*-style market, head over to the edges of the magnificent Mosque of Sayyidna Al Hussein. The cats who prefer a quieter setting may be nestled there, to escape the heat of the day. One thing street cats often lack is fresh water. Don't be shy about pouring a bit out from your bottle.

Mosque of Ibn Tulun

It's said that the prophet Mohammed had a cat named Muezza. One day, while he was dressing himself for prayer, the prophet noticed Muezza had fallen asleep on the sleeve of his robe. Rather than disturb the cat, Mohammed cut off the sleeve, and proceeded to dress as normal. This is the vibe you are walking into when you walk into a mosque.

Cats are considered pure animals in Islam. Thus, they are endowed with a freedom granted to virtually no other animal: the ability to enter mosques as guests rather than pests. Imams have been known to pause their lectures for a cat that has wandered in, offering scritches and a bit of food.

Most mosques in Cairo have resident cats. Step inside Al-Azhar, Cairo's venerated, 1000-year-old seat of Islamic leadership, and the pandemonium and grime of the city are immediately snuffed out, replaced by cool silence and a white floor so gleaming you have to squint to look at it. Many cats head here for quiet and safety – not so different from the humans, if you think about it.

However, Ibn Tulun is considered by many travelers to have the most reliable sighting of mosque cats. Sit inside its vast, sand-colored arcade, and it's very likely a cat will appear, strolling casually between the stone archways, or sunning itself on the hot, clean stones of the courtyard. Docents and imams here will sometimes provide straw mats for cats who are in distress or giving birth. The resident cats here are particularly well-fed and cared for by staff and worshippers alike, and tend to be extremely friendly.

LOCATION

Sharia Al Saliba, Sayeda Zeinab, Cairo.

SPECIAL NOTES

Prepare to remove your shoes, and women should plan to cover their hair and legs. Public visiting hours are generally from 9am to 4pm. The mosque holds prayer on Friday.

"Wait in line at the *local pita shop*, sit in the dusty red *glow of sunset* puffing a shisha, walk down the *shores of the inky Nile* next to the shaabi-blasting felucca boats, and a cat will almost certainly *cross your path.*"

Cats still reign in Cairo.

Temple of Bubastis

LOCATION

The archaeological site is on Sharia Al Shohaada, roughly 1.5 miles (2.4km) south of the Zagazig Railway Station. Ask taxi and tuk-tuk drivers for "Tell Basta."

SPECIAL NOTES

Tickets to the museum are E£150 (about $2.90), and the hours are usually 8am-5pm.

Imagine you are in ancient Egypt, sailing a barge along the Nile, bellowing raunchy songs, shouting insults at your neighbor, flashing skin, and getting absolutely trashed on wine. According to Greek historian Herodotus, this is what 700,000 Egyptians did when they flooded into the Bubastis every year to celebrate Bastet. These actions were said to appease the cat goddess.

Is it still possible to worship Bastet in her original temple? Not quite like that (at least, I wouldn't recommend it), but you can still go where it once happened.

Bastet got her start as a sun-drenched warrior goddess, her face that of a lioness. As the centuries progressed, her face evolved from lion to the house cat most of us recognize today (it's not that dissimilar an evolutionary path taken by actual domestic cats). The daughter of Ra and Isis, she would accompany her father through the sky before coming home to fight the evil snake Apep before bedtime. Between these duties, she also managed to take on the role of pregnancy guardian, fertility blesser, and protectress against infectious disease, home invasion and evil spirits. Statues in her likeness were often carved out of alabaster. She was, to put it mildly, a big deal.

Bastet's main temple was in Bubastis (sometimes called Tell Basta or Per Basta), whose foundations are still preserved in the Cairo suburb of Zagazig. This was the primary seat of the cult of Bastet, and it functioned as the capital of ancient Egypt during the 22nd dynasty.

Today, you can wander the stone remains of the actual temple (a bit surreal, with the city of Zagazig pressing in on all sides overhead). Then, head over to the Museum of Tal Basta Antiquities to see where most of the historic treasures currently live. The museum is young, having only opened in 2018, and it's much smaller than the grand ancient Egyptian museums in Cairo. However, its focus is mainly on Bastet and the people who lived and ruled in her city. Some of the artifacts here are large, some are small. Some are vases with reliefs of her glory; others are statuettes with amber eyes. Some of Bastet's avatars appear to be little more than bronze statues of common house cats, attesting to how similar the two truly came to be, visually.

Symbolically, you could argue that there is no real difference between the almighty daughter of Ra and the common strays you see when you step outside the museum, meowing hello.

Cats were highly revered in ancient Egypt.

CITY CATS

SAN FRANCISCO BAY AREA, CALIFORNIA, USA

San Francisco Bay Area

SAN FRANCISCO IS A pipsqueak as far as metropolises go. It houses fewer than a million people in its 7-mile-by-7-mile frame. But when combined with the surrounding counties, the entire place is known as the Bay Area. And the Bay Area loves cats.

Cat ownership is insanely common here; one in every three people in Santa Clara County considers themselves a cat parent. That's not to say feral colonies don't exist. But for its population density, the Bay Area has a lot to be proud of, cat-wise. Many TNR programs were pioneered here in the 1990s, and continue to be pursued by both organized charities and regular citizens who simply want to help out their neighborhoods.

A certified therapy cat named Duke Ellington may greet you at SFO airport, part of the Wag Brigade initiative to "make flying suck less." The Cat Man of West Oakland – a guy with a cat-themed batman logo who helps Oakland's "hoodcats" – sells gigantic catnip blunts and Pure Moods spoof albums to help your cat take better naps. The cats that live in the Bay Area are often as eclectic and ambitious as the human residents. When electric street cars were introduced to downtown San Francisco in the late 1800s, cats would apparently creep out at night after traffic had died down, and head to the rails to lick, roll and yowl in ecstasy from the thrill of the buzz.

Cat Town

LOCATION
2869 Broadway St, Oakland.

SPECIAL NOTES
They are open Thu-Sun, from 10am-5pm (last visit at 4pm). Reservations are recommended. It's $14 an hour per person, but visits are free on the first Thursday of each month.

Opened in 2014, in collaboration with The Cat Man of West Oakland, Cat Town is the first cat cafe in the US, and was founded with the express goal of helping elderly, stressed, and/or partially disabled cats get a better shot at adoption. This was done by keeping them out of cages. New, wary cats arrive in the airy cat lounge and learn how to let loose by observing the outgoing residents who have been there for a longer period of time. In 2017, after three years of operation and due to its raging popularity, Cat Town doubled its size, and now includes private rooms for cats with more specialized needs.

The unpretentious interior features cat trees shaped like local high-rises, (including the beloved Oakland Tribune Tower) and a gorgeous mural wall by a local street artist. Special events at night include cat yoga, cat cello serenades, cat board game night and even cat mini golf.

Cat Town is not just a cafe, but a nonprofit animal charity, staffed in large part by volunteers. It's the neighboring business that actually serves drinks: Souvenir, a sleek, friendly coffee shop brewing up some of the freshest, bespoke beans in the East Bay. Cat Town offers other local nonprofits and community groups a handful of free visits each year – because they understand happy cats make for a happy community, and vice versa.

TACOS POR LOS GATOS
SUSHI

FISH QUEEN
Spiced SARDINES
Sardinoj
BEL PESCE
SARDE
SARDE
PICCANTI
SARDE
Yummy
Melhor!
Melhor!

KitTea Cat Lounge

If there was such a thing as a cat spa, I imagine it would have all the options you can currently find at KitTea Cat Lounge. This is the city of San Francisco's only official cat cafe, and they take the job incredibly seriously.

KitTea isn't so much a cafe as a kind of perpetual, cat-themed group therapy session. They have 20 permanent cats (officially making them a sanctuary), in addition to a host of adoptable cats. They also host a regular lineup of cat-themed movie nights, cat yoga sessions, cat-themed paint-and-sips, cat lounge cello concerts, and cat-accompanied sound baths. It's the "Purrlates" that really seems to have put them on the map, though.

On varying Wednesday and Friday evenings, you can reserve a spot at a 60-minute Pilates class that takes place in the plushy, mod lounge space. Bring a mat, a water bottle, and a T-shirt – or better yet, long sleeves – as the cats have a tendency to hop on bending backs and clamber over flexing tummies. The final 20 minutes of the class are reserved for sipping sparkling wine, shopping in the cat-themed gift shop, and cuddling the kitties that have spent the last 40 minutes jumping all over you.

LOCATION

1266 Valencia St, San Francisco.

SPECIAL NOTES

Reservations are required and run about $30 an hour. That includes a drink, and while there's no food, outside snacks are allowed. The latest schedule of classes and events is at kitteasf.com.

"The cats that *live* in the Bay Area are often as *eclectic and ambitious* as the *human residents.*"

An outdoorsy cat living its best life in the Bay Area.

Mini Cat Town

LOCATION
2200 Eastridge Loop Space 1076, San Jose.

SPECIAL NOTES
It's walk-in only, typically in 30-minute chunks. A waitlist can build up on weekends around 2pm. Outside drinks are allowed, but no food is permitted in the cat lounge - these little guys would probably try to eat anything.

If there is a King Kong of cat cafes in the Bay Area, it's Mini Cat Town. The flagship is in San Jose's Eastridge Mall, but they have five locations across the entire region, from Palo Alto to Santa Rosa.

Mini Cat Town was founded by Thi, Tram and Thoa Bui, three sisters in South San Jose, where stray cats are notoriously, ah, busy. The kids did their best to nurture the constant wave of kittens popping out from bushes, hiding under cars and wandering into the street, giving them shelter and food, and adopting them out to neighbors as often as possible. But the problem kept, well, breeding. The girls learned TNR, and took jobs at Baskin-Robbins to pay for traps and food, until all hundred or so cats in their neighborhood had been fixed.

That kind of drive doesn't evaporate overnight, apparently. Now adults, the sisters have gone corporate. They founded Mini Cat Town in 2015 – a cat lounge whose primary focus is on kittens. At first that might seem like a cheap pander ("what about the older cats who need love, too?"), but the truth is, thousands of abandoned neonatal kittens flood local shelters every spring. And, because they are adorable and impressionable, humans love to play with them. Really, Mini Cat Town is just a broker of kitten joy, transporting tiny fluffballs from the street to your lap. Unsurprisingly, their adoption rate is insanely high, with over 3000 total adoptions to date.

KITTENS
ADOPTED

CAT-TOPIAS

Cat-Topias

MAJOR CITIES ARE A reliable place to see domestic cats. We evolved together in them. Cats help with pest control and give humans something to do with their tuna cans. But there are certain places on Earth where cats and humans converge beyond the skyscrapers and back alleys – places that rival what a major city can offer, as if a great feline deity pointed their finger on a map and said “here.”

These cat-topias, as we call them, usually fall outside of city limits, and so might require a bit more effort and planning to visit. Some of them require great adventure: sailing to sparsely populated islands, fording mountain passes to remote medieval villages, or going to New Jersey. Be sure to check mass transit schedules ahead of time, and make sure the last boat doesn’t leave without you (literally).

Garden State Cat Club Expo

LOCATION
The Expo is typically held at the Sheraton Hotel, 125 Raritan Center Pkwy, Edison, New Jersey.

SPECIAL NOTES
This event is usually held on the third weekend of July. Admission fees vary, starting at $15. Visit gardenstatecatexpo.com for more information.

For when safaris feel too expansive, and cat cafes feel too limited. The Garden State Cat Club of NJ, Inc.'s annual Expo in New Jersey hosts several thousand human guests and hundreds of cats together in one gigantic room, and getting in costs less than a two-hour visit at most cat cafes. This is the highest potency-to-price dose of cats you can find on the Eastern seaboard.

The Expo is complete with agility tests for cats, a parade of breeds, a costume contest, a universe of vendors hawking every kind of cat trinket imaginable, and, of course, a plethora of gifts for your own precious fluff-ling. If you have yet to be blessed by the Cat Distribution System, the Expo also hosts several local shelters showcasing adoptable cats. Since house pets can be entered into event competitions, you could adopt a fur baby one year and show her off as your darling diva the next. (They also prohibit any cat entered in any competition from being declawed, which is a testament to their commitment to cat joy.)

The Expo is the primary fundraiser for the Garden State Cat Club. When you consider that they accept food donations for rescues, the club has likely brought over $200,000 worth of aid to the cats of America's East Coast since 1982. There are a handful of festivals similar in size and scope to the Garden State Cat Club's Expo. Check out Los Angeles' CatCon, or the POP Cats art and cat show, which hosts a series of conventions throughout the US. In Canada, you can explore MeowFest (held alternately in Vancouver and Toronto) and Edmonton Cat Festival. In Australia, the Cat Lovers Festival is the country's largest feline festival.

5th
BEST
Cat in
CFA
Sponsored
by

BUKO

De Poezenboot (Cat Boat)

Cats have a long history as fishermen's best friend – chasing rodents away from the daily catch and keeping a ship's cargo safe while far out at sea.

The cats on the Poezenboot, however, have engaged in a kind of mutiny, overtaking the boat completely.

Technically a houseboat, the Poezenboot was the brainchild of Henriette van Weelde back in 1966. She gained a neighborhood reputation for being the lady who would always help a stray. Soon enough, a stray became *every* stray, and her house was overrun. Even cat ladies have their limits. In response, Henriette commandeered a retired Dutch sailing barge, contracted some renovations, and brought the cats aboard. Content in the fresh air and sunshine, they stayed.

Over a few decades, the Poezenboot was upgraded to a houseboat specially renovated for the needs of several cats, and even once had its own newspaper. At one point, it was a fleet of two vessels, but the local government refused to grant a license for the second boat on the grounds that it wasn't a tourist attraction.

Today, the Poezenboot is a single floating vessel of cat fur on the Amsterdam canals, serving not just as a cat sanctuary, but an adoption center, TNR program hub, and low-cost veterinary resource center. They do this without any funding from the local government, surviving on donors alone.

LOCATION

Singel 38 G,
1015 AB, Amsterdam,
The Netherlands

SPECIAL NOTES

The boat is docked close to Amsterdam Central station. Only six humans are allowed on board at a time, between 1pm and 3pm, on Tuesday, Friday and Saturday. If that seems draconian, then you try running a boat manned only by cats. Updated schedules can be found at depoezenboot.nl

Kotor

LOCATION
Montenegro.

You can fly into Dubrovnik, Croatia, and take a ferry, bus or car to Kotor. It's also a popular cruise port.

The ancient Dalmatian city-state of Kotor has gained fame as a UNESCO World Heritage Site and a popular modern cruise port. Arguably, however, Kotor's largest claim to fame is its cats. This place could be described as the world's largest cat cafe – just open-air, and with a medieval village theme.

The famous Old Town is a maze of terra-cotta roofs, Mediterranean palm trees and stone ramparts, guarded over by towering limestone cliffs. Venetian fortress walls hold back the teal and sapphire waters of the Adriatic. It's the stuff of pure fantasy. And every corner you turn, a posse of cats is there, just waiting to ignore you. No one is quite sure how many felines actually live here, but when you ask the locals, the most common response is "hundreds." Here, cats are considered auspicious and the whole town sees their care as a bit of a collective responsibility.

When exactly cats became such a symbol of good luck is a matter of some debate. Kotor served as a port city to a succession of colonizers, from the Romans, to the Byzantines to the Venetians. Globe-crossing ships would dock in the Bay of Kotor, and their feline sailors would hop straight off into town on shore leave. This was perhaps best illustrated by the 1918 Cattaro Mutiny, when a group of mistreated Slavic sailors mutinied against their Austro-Hungarian overlords. The sailors docked their ships in protest, and cats flooded into the town, perhaps, symbolically carrying the idea of rebellion on their paws. It also probably helped that they immediately began gobbling up snakes and rats that would descend into the town from the surrounding mountains.

The cats of Kotor are considered part of the attraction, along with the architecture and historic backdrops. Hundreds of plump and healthy felines

Souvenir OLD TOWN
Cats shop
Hand made
MONTENEGRO

roam the streets freely, fed on leftover morsels of Montenegrin delicacies like milk-braised lamb, marinated squid and local sausage. You can catch a row of whiskers snoozing on a slab of sunbaked rampart, flitting from cafe to cafe for a fresh snack, or playing in the shade of the green bushes that decorate the fortress walls.

Although the cats are supported by a few official groups (including Kotor Kitties charity and the local cat museum), the entire town pitches in to help, often inviting them in as temporary roommates during the colder months. As such, these are some of the least shy stray cats you'll ever encounter. Grab a glass of Montenegrin wine and bask in the sun together.

SPECIAL NOTES

There are a number of cat-themed souvenir shops and boutiques celebrating the local cats, but the Cats Museum donates a portion of its profits to feeding the cats. Kotor Kitties has embarked on a TNR mission to ensure the cat population stays charmingly large, and not out of control. If you have extra euros to spare before leaving town, the museum is a good place to donate.

Cats aren't "strays" in the village of Kotor but more like friendly neighbors. Who everyone lets sleep on store shelves.

"This place could be described as the *world's largest cat cafe* – just open-air, and with a *medieval village* theme."

A guardian of Kotor's medieval walls enjoys the sea air, preparing for another round of tourist adoration.

Heather's Hale
Karen's House

Lāna`i Cat Sanctuary

In the middle of the 18th century, cats scampered off trading ships and onto the so-called Sandwich Islands, in the middle of the Pacific Ocean. Initially, the locals were charmed by these furry newcomers. Then, the cats began murdering the birds – hundreds and hundreds of them (the poor things were easy prey, having not co-evolved with any feline predators). TNR programs were finally introduced in the late 20th century, to tame the growth of 100 generations of seafaring cats who quite literally had nowhere else to go – unless they wanted to sprout gills and wander into the sea. But it was hardly enough.

Lāna`i is a Hawaiian island that few tourists venture to visit. For many years, there was basically nowhere to go: it was a coast-to-coast pineapple farm. That was until the island's owners realized they could make far more money luring tourists to the shores of a lesser-visited paradise than they could from slinging Maui Golds to the mainland. Now, the island hosts a handful of breathtaking hotels, a premier golf course, and the single greatest collection of *Felis catus* in the Pacific Ocean.

The sanctuary really began in 2004, when local resident Kathy Carroll felt a *kuleana* (a Hawaiian call of duty) to take care of the bedraggled feline population on Lāna`i. Every Hawaiian island contains an abundance of stray cats (Maui is estimated to have half a million alone), but there is usually at least one vet to help care for them. Lāna`i had nothing: no veterinarian, shelter, or rescue group to speak of.

LOCATION

Lāna`i Island, Hawaii, USA.

Lāna`i has one tiny airport. Most people opt to take the hour-long foot ferry from Maui, then rent a car on Lāna`i for the half-hour drive to the sanctuary. Be sure to check the schedule at go-lanai.com before you set out.

SPECIAL NOTES

The Sanctuary is open to the public from 9am-3pm every day of the year.

If you've always dreamed of a Hawaiian wedding but thought "the only thing missing is 700 cats," good news - they do weddings.

Admission is free. The Lāna`i Cat Sanctuary subsists (somewhat miraculously) on donations only. However, getting there is far from cheap. Be sure to check the ferry prices from Maui over to Lāna`i, which typically run about $120 roundtrip for non-locals. That's before the car or shuttle you have to rent to get from the ferry dock to the west side of the island; Lāna`i has no public transportation to speak of. The whole trip can easily cost $300.

The Lāna`i Cat Sanctuary started in a horse barn, then advanced to 4 barren acres (2 hectares) on the island's west side, which were loved and coaxed into a "purradise." Today, stacks of wooden cat condos and colorful platforms are laid out over grassy fields punctuated by leis and sprays of banana leaves. Look up into the branches of the giant mango tree and you'll see about as many cat bellies as you do tropical fruits. These are all cats that would likely otherwise be killed (or be killers) in areas where native and endangered ground-nesting birds reside.

Under the leadership of Keoni Vaughn, the sanctuary gives each cat an individualized healthcare plan, ensuring every one is as comfortable as possible. The sanctuary has brought in more than 1800 cats since 2014, nearly half of whom have been adopted out.

Still, if you happen to have a few extra dollars on you before you depart back home, be sure to donate them to the sanctuary.

The Sanctuary started in a horse barn, and now makes up 4 acres (2 hectares) of paradise for Hawaii's lost seafaring cats.

"...stacks of wooden *cat condos* and *colorful platforms* are laid out over *grassy fields* punctuated by *leis* and sprays of *banana leaves*."

Lounging around in Lāna'i

Kuching

LOCATION
Borneo, Malaysia.

Kuching is Borneo's third-largest city, with its own airport, so getting there is relatively easy compared to other far-flung "cat villages."

In the mid-20th century, the British colonial government decided it would be a good idea to spray gallons upon gallons of DDT into the jungles of Malaysian Borneo to kill malaria-ridden mosquitoes and rats. This public chemical bath had (surprise!) unintended consequences: the cat population plummeted, and the rat population cheerfully climbed. Humankind was invited to learn a lesson about applying blankets of chemicals to entire ecosystems, and in 1960, the British Air Force cooked up a scheme to fix the problem: Borneo needed more cats. Depending on whose version of the story you believe, anywhere from 23 to 14,000 cats were airlifted from Singapore into Borneo – an endeavor very precisely named Operation Cat Drop. The hungry cats happily feasted on the free buffet of rats, and balance was more or less returned to the jungle.

Borneo tempts most animal-loving visitors with the promise of an orangutan sighting in its natural habitat. The brilliant, shy apes may be the stars of the island, but there is one major city that has decided to rebel and dedicate itself entirely to an obsession with cats: Kuching.

"Everywhere I looked I saw felines," wrote Esme Fox for BBC.co.uk in 2022. "A giant white cat waved at me from a roundabout just outside Chinatown. A family of robot-like cats stared from the side of the road close to a mosque. Spray-painted alley cats slunk around the sides of buildings in the form of street art." Residents tune into the local radio station Cats FM. The city's crest, floating atop a grand pillar, is a justice scale and a golden cat

SEDC
coway
PINJAM
TEO HOE HIN

waving its paw, with four white cats guarding the base. The Kuching Cat Museum is a veritable temple of feline kitsch and iconography, stuffed with everything from Egyptian cat mummies to delicate porcelain figurines. Every September, the Kuching International Cat Festival takes over the waterfront.

This really is "cat town" – even the word *kucing* means cat in the Malay language. But why has the devotion become so intense here? Some theorize it's due to Kuching's diverse human population, comprising Malay, Chinese, Indian, Iban, Bidayuh, Orang Ulu and Melanu people. These groups have one thing in common: they treasure cats, either as a symbol of good luck, the beloved pet of a prophet, or simply as the world's most adorable pest control.

Curiously, there are mixed reports of how many real, live cats you'll actually see in Kuching. Some visitors claim tenderhearted cafe owners are often spotted handing out free scraps to strays. Other visitors claim they couldn't find any real cats at all. Not every person in Kuching loves cats, and there have been varied efforts to care for the strays that wander around after Operation Cat Drop. Great work has been done by the Love Kuching Project, Pawsitive Vibes Foundation, and other community stewardship societies.

Your most reliable cat fix is at Meow Meow Cat Cafe, a modest coffee shop overlooking the Sarawak river, that's home to around six resident cats. Unlike most cat cafes in the world, you don't need an appointment to visit Meow Meow. You can lounge on the couch next to a purring pile of fluff or wave a string in front of a hypnotized kitten more or less from opening until closing.

SPECIAL NOTES

Meow Meow seems to be the favorite cat cafe, but Catfe Cafe will also happily shower you in caffeine and cat fur.

A Kuching cat, presumably staring around the corner at yet another statue of (what else?) itself.

"The Kuching Cat Museum is a *veritable temple* of *feline kitsch* and *iconography*, stuffed with everything from *Egyptian cat mummies* to delicate porcelain figurines."

Cats are a symbol of local pride and luck in Kuching, after hundreds of them were dropped into the city to clear out a pest problem.

50
CAUTION
KINO

Parque Kennedy

Most big city parks have a stray cat population. But few stray cats are as pampered as those in Peru's Parque Kennedy.

Situated in the posh Miraflores neighborhood, Parque Kennedy is the unofficial town square of Lima and a must-stop for any tourist – with its regal collection of emerald lawns, swept sidewalks, and manicured troops of flowers. Painters perch on benches, attempting to capture the muse of daily life; singers' voices echo among the trees; and food vendors perfume the air with aromas of sweet-potato donuts, warm sausages, and corn spiced with cloves.

The cats who live here are about as well-kept as the gardens. A dish of food and water rests at the base of most trees. The local government keeps detailed accounts of population size and sanitary conditions, and the cats' healthcare is managed by Grupo Voluntario de Defensa Felina (which also spearheads the park's TNR program and the occasional adoption). There is a small feline hotel, where the cats take their nightly rest. It's unclear exactly how many cats live in the park, but one visitor describes it as being like an Easter egg hunt trying to spot them all. Frequently, it's not even referred to as Parque Kennedy at all, but as "El Parque de los Gatos" (cat park).

Like most other cities with large groups of strays, the theory goes that Parque Kennedy's cats were originally introduced to take care of plague-carrying rats (possibly by the priests of a nearby church). After rapidly dismantling the rodent problem, the cats quickly charmed the locals. Today, many consider it something of a free animal therapy zone; there's no need to

LOCATION

Lima, Peru.

There is a 50-minute direct train from Lima Airport to Parque Kennedy. Berlín bus stop, located right across from the park, serves numerous bus lines throughout the city.

SPECIAL NOTES

Parque Kennedy is open 24 hours and is encircled by some of Lima's best cafes, restaurants and shopping. If you're heading there, be sure to leave time to stroll the nearby streets and explore the art vendors.

fight with your landlord about your right to own a cat when you can get your feline fix and your nature fix down the road at the same time.

Having been treated so well most of their lives, Parque Kennedy's cats are some of the friendliest strays you'll ever meet. They perch in sunny flower beds, scramble up tree trunks, lounge next to strangers on park benches, and are generally responsive to a "pspspsps." Many are quite eager to hop into your lap and purr the afternoon away for a few hours while you read or chat with a friend. Thoughtfully, there are also a few fenced-off areas for the cats to retreat to, in the event that they tire of public adoration.

In Parque Kennedy, it's downright hard to find a flowerbed without a pair of cat ears in it.

Japanese Cat Islands

LOCATION
Tashirojima, Japan.

Tashirojima is only accessible by a ferry. There are two departing ports in Ishinomaki and two arrival ports on Tashirojima. Chūō is said to be the easier departing port, and Nitoda is rumored to have a higher cat population.

If you've ever wanted to be on a desert island surrounded by nothing but cats, Japan has you covered. There are at least ten *neko no shima* (cat islands) in the nation's domain – that is, places cats outnumber humans. By a lot.

Japan's *neko no shima* are tiny islands typically classified as "terminal villages" – meaning most of the population is over 65, there is no major commercial industry, the roads are questionable at best, and nobody wants to move in. Recognizing that this is some people's idea of heaven, a few islands have built tourist infrastructure. But even this is quite limited.

Almost universally, cats were first brought to places that would later be known as "cat islands" as pest control, successfully keeping rodents away from storehouses, fishnets, and even delicate silkworms. Facing no cars or natural predators, and served by an adoring public that considered them to be good luck, the cats more or less took over. I mean, really took over. As of this writing, 80 cats call Aoshima Island home, compared to four humans – presumably living at the apex of introverted cat lady bliss. Aoshima is worth putting on your cat-travel list if for no other reason than that its clock is running out. In a remarkable example of TNR success, every single cat here has been fixed. This means there will soon be no more cats (and, likely, no more humans) left, so pet them while they're still purring.

Aoshima is one mere example, but Japan's main cat island is probably Tashirojima – a gorgeous, green nugget of an island off the Miyagi coast. The human-to-cat ratio is slightly better here than in Aoshima, but not by

much: 61 humans to 130 felines. The 61 humans seem to take their role as caretakers of a *neko no shima* very seriously. Dogs are not permitted. Guests can stay in cat-themed lodges. There is a cat shrine in the forested center of the island. In sum, if cat lady heaven were real, Tashirojima would be an excellent model for it.

The cats here have really been in charge since the Edo period, supporting sericulturists and fishermen. They were also said to predict ocean weather and reveal fishing patterns (how exactly they did this is a mystery, but who am I to tell a fisherman he can't use a cat as a crystal ball). Cats have even been credited with keeping the majority of the island from being destroyed during the 2011 Tōhoku earthquake and tsunami. A vet visits twice a month.

Tashirojima's famous cat shrine – about a half-mile walk from Ōdomari Port – is a humble little thing, tucked into the trees and surrounded by forest stones. The shrine was originally built to commemorate a cat who was accidentally killed by a rock-collecting fisherman. Filled with remorse, the fisherman threw the beloved stray a funeral. Today, the shrine is a place where humans offer cat toys and figurines, and the cats nearby are notoriously friendly. There have even been reports of belly rubs.

Perhaps one of the nicest aspects of visiting Tashirojima – or any *neko no shima* – is how friendly the cats are. Even while effectively living as strays, they have been protected and cared for their entire lives and so associate humans with affection and treats. It can be a surreal experience if you are used to frightened city cats and fearful rescues, staring at you from under bushes and staircases. These guys will probably be excited to see you.

SPECIAL NOTES

On Tashirojima, the cats are fed daily at noon at Shima no Eki, if you want to see a mass gathering. There is a cafe and vending machine there as well, but that's about it for shops. If you want to stay the night, Tashirojima is also home to a cluster of cottages (topped with cat ears, of course) outfitted with artwork by beloved manga artists such as Chiba Tetsuya, Ishinomori Shotaro, and Kimura Naomi. If you're planning to stay, reservations are recommended.

Cats in Tashirojima are friendly--at least to people that visit.

"Guests can stay in *cat-themed lodges.* There is a *cat shrine* in the forested center of the *island.* In sum, if *cat lady heaven* were real, Tashirojima would be an *excellent* model for it."

A cat in Aoshima sleeps soundly knowing its being well taken care of.

Shanghai Cat Island

Shanghai's "Cat Island" is a bit of a misnomer – the original site was on a lush, semi-rural island in the Pudong district of Shanghai but had to be moved to the mainland's Baoshan district. Nonetheless, the tall trees and open courtyard of the new facility have a similar calming effect that morphs into whimsy and excitement when brightly colored murals, statues and hand-decorated cat houses come into view. Cat Island may not be a proper, ocean-locked island, but if you want to get lost in a sea of fluff and toe beans, this is the place.

The other name for Shanghai Cat Island is actually "Homeless Cat Island." Pets didn't become popular with China's modern middle class until around the 1990s. Because of this, many perfectly loving pet parents are forced by circumstances to surrender their pets. That used to look like putting your pet out on the street and then leaving town. It's heartbreaking, but this is why Cat Island is crucial for the Shanghai stray cat community. Not only because there are an estimated minimum of 400,000 stray cats in Shanghai, but if your job relocates you to a city where you can't find a pet-friendly apartment, you might have to make the difficult decision to turn them out – or, you can bring them here.

The island was originally founded by Zha Zhenliang, and day-to-day operations are overseen by Chen Hao, the sanctuary manager. All the cats here are fixed, vaccinated, and cared for by a series of volunteers. Funding for all of this food and medical care comes from a combination of the

LOCATION

Shanghai, China

62 Shengzhai Zhongxinzhai, Gucun Town, Baoshan District, Shanghai.

Limited parking is available, but public transportation is recommended.

SPECIAL NOTES
Cat Island is open 10am-4pm Tue-Fri, 10am-5pm Sat & Sun. Reservations are required, and there's a daily visitor cap, so consider booking early. Minors must be accompanied by an adult, and children under 12 are not allowed. Note that from July 1 to August 31, the island is only open to visitors at night (likely to accommodate the cats' proclivity to snooze through the daytime heat).

Shanghai Yicai Feiyang Public Welfare Foundation and the Pudong New Area Cohesion Foundation, as well as heaps of small donations from visitors. Admission comes at the jaw-droppingly generous cost of "free."

In addition to the rescue and adoption facilities, Cat Island has an education center that has been bridging the gaps in understanding for a community that wants to harmoniously coexist with their feline neighbors, including how people can begin their own TNR programs in other neighborhoods across China.

After touring the space, you can unwind in a spacious outdoor lounge or hit up the cafe and reflect on the idea of adopting one of these homeless cats.

A cat takes a stroll through the Baoshan district.

BIG CATS

SANCTUARIES

Big Cats: Sanctuaries

IF YOU PICKED UP this book, you have probably fantasized at some point in your life about owning a big cat. Or, maybe not owning, but perhaps...befriending. Cohabitating? At least, brunching together on waffles and raw ostrich (respectively). There is something extraordinarily flattering about a member of *Felis catus* choosing to spend time with you. Multiply that feeling by 400 pounds, and that's how it would feel to hang out with anyone from the genus *Panthera.*

That feeling is probably what compels starry-eyed tourists to spend thousands of dollars on safari hotels, where lion cubs snuggle with you as you watch the sunset. Behind the curtain of these coveted experiences are (sorry to have to tell you this) drugged or murdered mother cats, adult cats that can never return home, and worse. When we participate in experiences like this, we are fueling the exploitation of creatures that we forget are more than symbols. They are highly intelligent apex animals that do not crave nor require domestication.

For as long as people have been admiring big cats, there has been an unfortunate, consequential motivation for other humans to poach them. Sometimes, these cats escape or are rescued from captivity. But they are unable to return to their homelands, caught somewhere between wild and domesticated. Fortunately, many of them can still live happy, healthy lives.

This book doesn't recommend hotels where you can pet jaguars, or highlight private zoos where anxious cheetahs pace tiny enclosures. Instead, you'll find places that operate as true sanctuaries for big cats, prioritizing the health and wellness of the animals above the human desire to give them gigantic hugs. As such, some of these places are only open to the public under special circumstances. Some don't allow young children, and some only allow you to see the cats from hundreds of feet in the air.

So, yes, compared to the dreamy idea of visiting a tiger petting zoo, these parks and centers may fall short. But they put the actual animal first, and that's what ultimately makes them so great. They still allow regular humans to come and admire a big cat without having to worry if that very desire is being used to harm said cat. I know I would rather experience the lightning thrill of glimpsing a wildcat wandering through its natural home, versus staring at it from a cage.

Every listing here is accredited for its ethics, and regularly vetted. Organizations like GFAS (Global Federation of Animal Sanctuaries) and BCSA (Big Cat Sanctuary Alliance) maintain updated listings of private sanctuaries that meet their strict standards. These are places that focus on providing happy lives and high-quality veterinary care for rescued cats, as well as helping to eliminate commercial animal trade and abusive private ownership.

We hope you enjoy visiting them and keeping the love a two-way street for both humans and cats.

Raja, an African Caracal who lives at the Wildcat Ridge Sanctuary in Oregon.

ARCAS Wildlife Rescue Center

LOCATION
Petén, Guatemala.

ARCAS is on Lake Petén Itza (conveniently, or perhaps ironically, right next to the Peténcito Zoo), and is primarily reached by boat. You can grab a water taxi from Flores or San Miguel, for around Q200 (about $26).

The Maya Biosphere Reserve is a vast, protected Eden of tropical trees, ancient stone temples, and all manner of chirping, squawking and roaring wildlife. It's one of the world's largest and most important rainforests, taking up one-fifth of Guatemala, thanks in large part to local citizens who were fed up with the ravages of clear cutting, deforestation and energy extraction, and instead sought to reclaim their country's inherent majesty.

The forest is a haven for howler monkeys, camouflaging crocodiles, neon tree frogs, and candy-colored birds. But if you're a cat lover, you're here for the star: the jaguar – the largest cat native to the Americas, with the notable distinction of how it kills. A jaguar simply plops out of the tree canopy before you can blink, and sinks its massive fangs directly through the skull of its prey (we can only imagine this is what your Mr. Paws back at home thinks is happening when he air-dives onto his catnip mouse).

The Maya Biosphere Reserve struck a deal with humans: if you stay out of the rainforest's re-growth, we will build a few places where you can get close enough to truly admire it, so you'll be inspired to let it grow further. This is where the ARCAS Wildlife Rescue Center comes in.

ARCAS was founded in 1989 to protect the Maya forest's wildlife from hunters seeking stock for the illegal exotic pet trade. Its first move was to construct a wildlife rescue center, in order to care for those wild animals that had been rescued from poachers, but could not yet be released into the wild without, well…defeating the entire point of the rescue. As time went on, the

BIENVENIDOS
ARCAS

rescue center also became a beacon for wildlife emergencies and human education, saving animals at risk of habitat loss due to excessive logging, farmland development and oil exploration. They currently care for somewhere between 300 and 600 endangered animals per year.

Since most of the animals staying at ARCAS Petén are destined to return to the wild, they are not available for public viewing, and unlike many other "rescue centers," they do not have cages stacked like townhouses down long aisles of human sidewalks. Instead, rehabilitation enclosures are scattered throughout the jungle, in order to reduce stress on the animals, build their muscles, and re-accustom them to their natural environment – the rainforest. The staff are at the forefront of the science of releasing animals back into the wild.

However, there are a few animals whose return to the wild would spell certain doom, and so now live at ARCAS full time – surrounded by humans who are more or less obsessed with keeping them in a state of contentedness.

The public part of the compound begins with a climb up a set of stone steps, reminiscent of the Mayan ruins scattered inside the surrounding jungle. There is a small exhibition explaining ARCAS's work, a museum, and outdoor public walkways leading to the royal residents of the Central American rainforest. The cats here include jaguars, but also jaguarundi, ocelots, pumas and margays. The front of each animal's large enclosure displays a QR code that tells the animal's story, including the details of how it came to be brought to ARCAS. You're here for the cats, of course, but consider a polite nod to the parrots, macaws, toucans, spider monkeys and crocodiles that live here as well.

SPECIAL NOTES

The center is open daily 8am-4:30pm with an entrance fee of Q35 (around $5).

ARCAS is an animal welfare flagship, where wildlife-specialist veterinarians come from all over the world to intern, volunteer, and sharpen their skills. If you are interested in volunteering, they have applications on their website year-round.

Most of the animals at ARCAS are only here for a short while, rehabilitating in enclosures deep inside the rainforest.

WildCat Ridge Sanctuary

Mountain lions are the big cat most associated with North America; they are the only native big cats found up there. However, hidden in the dewy, evergreen hills of central Oregon, there is a sanctuary of big cats so astounding in its breadth, you'll think you've died and gone to wildcat heaven.

WildCat Ridge Sanctuary is home to a panoply of lesser feline lords like caracals, hybrids and servals, all the way up to reps of the royal family: lions, tigers and cheetahs. There's also about 20 domestic cats. And some dogs. Oh, and cows, sheep, pigs, chickens and a couple of donkeys (you can almost imagine the owners sighing an exasperated "we've gone this far, why not?" and throwing another rescue into the mix). In total, over 80 animals live here.

Why so much diversity? WildCat Ridge caters exclusively (and sadly) to animals born in captivity, most of whom were subjected to abuse, neglect, or botched attempts at human care. This makes them what is known as a "last hope" sanctuary, since these felines have no ability to survive in the wild. Due to their history, many of the exotic cats will not tolerate being touched by humans. And for the owners and workers, that's just fine. There is no insisting on snuggling here. The sanctuary's philosophy is adamantly hands-off, in part due to founder Cheryl Tuller.

Tuller believes that many curious, perhaps even well-meaning, humans take on the care of wildcats or hybrid cats completely forgetting that they are, in fact, wild animals. She knows because, in 1996, she did that very thing, adopting a hybrid cat named BoBo, who absolutely insisted on

LOCATION
Oregon, USA.

Due to privacy concerns, the exact address of the sanctuary is not viewable until you book a tour. However, the closest town is Scotts Mills, Oregon, between Portland and Salem.

SPECIAL NOTES
Tours typically take place June-September, when the weather is nice.

You can't stay overnight. Yes, even though you're booking your tour through Airbnb.There are a small handful of hotels and vacation rentals in nearby Scotts Mills and the surrounding towns.

refusing to enjoy life in the Oregon suburbs. She couldn't let him loose on the community, lest he embark upon a murder-suicide killing spree. Eventually, Tuller founded the Sanctuary – in part to give BoBo a proper outdoor home.

For the other, non-cat animals, the logic was simple: for every majestic big cat that needed rescuing, there were hundreds of less glamorous mammals who were about to be put on the chopping block, or were otherwise deemed "non-adoptable." Tuller and her team swooped in and took them here to live out a peaceful life – WildCat Ridge is, in many respects, an actual version of "a farm upstate."

But you're here for the cats. The catch with WildCat Ridge is that, as part of taking their role so seriously as a hand-off sanctuary, they are not – strictly speaking – open to the public in a "show up and buy a ticket" kind of way. The only way to get in is to book a private day tour (currently offered only through Airbnb Experiences). The bonus, however, is that you won't have to hustle and compete with other tourists. The downside is it costs about $500, is limited to parties of two to four, and permits no children under 14. If that seems a steep price tag, consider that it costs the Sanctuary $800,000 a year to operate, and that none of its full-time residents work or pay rent (because they are cats).

The tour takes you through 80 acres (32 hectares) of emerald Oregon meadows, including "Hybrid Haven," where hybrid cats romp and play in large arenas of lush greenery. The big cats are typically held in their own vast, private enclosures, and can often be caught napping in the sun, swatting at their toys, or burrowing in the many bushes of grass, silently watching you approach.

MiLA the Bengal cat, a cross between an Asian Leopard cat and a domestic cat.

The Wild Animal Sanctuary

LOCATION
Colorado, USA

2999 Co Rd 53,
Keenesburg.

SPECIAL NOTES
The Sanctuary is open from 9am to sunset year-round. Adult tickets run about $50. Check out their Wild Nights programs for better sightings during the summer months.

Most wildlife sanctuaries of upstanding repute face a conundrum: they want to share the majesty of exotic animals in their care, but they also can't expose those animals to humans too much, or the word *sanctuary* starts to lose its teeth. How do you let the humans see the wild animals without the wild animals seeing the humans?

The Wild Animal Sanctuary has come up with an ingenious method – 1.5 miles (2.4km) of sky-high wooden parapet. The humans walk across and look out over the animals. The animals go about their business, prowling happily in the Colorado grasslands and, apparently, never looking up (or, at least, don't consider anything floating that high in the air to be part of their territory). This is how the Sanctuary has earned the crown of "largest carnivore sanctuary in the world," managing almost 200,000 gawking humans per year while keeping their human-hating residents stress-free and cage-free. In short: if you're looking for the best glimpse at apex African and Asian felines without the cost of an international safari – this is probably this place.

The Sanctuary spans about 1400 acres (567 hectares) of Rocky Mountain grasslands, divided into 90 unique habitats where roughly 500 exotic animals reside. This grants each animal an "enclosure" footprint that most sanctuaries only dream of: up to 300 acres (121 hectares) of their own kingdom. Tigers can hang out with tigers. Lions can hang out with lions. Jaguars can hang out alone, because they hate other jaguars. Every big cat you've ever dreamed

about is here. But there's also everything from grizzlies to wolves to emus lurking around in this predator megalopolis.

Like most places of this nature, the sanctuary acquired most of their animals under tragic circumstances. Many were transferred here by law enforcement after raids on abusive circuses or neglectful private owners (like the Tiger King). For some of these animals, their first steps onto this Colorado plain represents the first time they've felt grass underfoot. A large part of the sanctuary's work is teaching animals who have been raised in motherless captivity how to do things like meet others of their own species, engage in natural instincts like hunting and playing, and even how to run.

When you first walk into the welcome center in Keenesburg, it feels like you're walking into an airplane hangar that was turned into a strip mall by an animal-obsessed child. There are enough amenities here to make a major city zoo blush, from a massive ice cream shop to a Toys "R" Us-sized gift store. In other words, the sanctuary is designed to handle the volume of people it attracts. But depart from the shopping mall, and you'll find yourself in the air, floating above a series of mammalian royalty – unparalleled possibly anywhere on Earth – roaming habitats that are as close to the wild as they could possibly get, short of being born there.

SPECIAL NOTES

Adjacent to the Wild Animal Sanctuary is the Wild Animal Refuge. They sound similar, but are very different. When the sanctuary hit "no vacancy," the refuge was developed, an additional whopping 9000 acres (3642 hectares) of habitat for the exotic, large mammals that kept pouring in after rescue raids. The refuge is, unfortunately, closed to the public (unless you can make one of the few donor-only events they host each year). *Try* to be content with your 1.5-mile (2.4km) skywalk over at the sanctuary.

A disapproving tiger at The Wild Animal Sanctuary in Colorado.

Rescate's Lifetime Care Sanctuary

Central America is home to superstar cats like jaguars and mountain lions, but also lesser-known jungle cats, some so small they would barely top the weight of your cat back home. These include elusive jaguarundi, who sometimes hunt with their best friends; tree-hopping margays; lanky ocelots; and golden oncilla, whose kitten-like faces practically make you ache.

Just about all of these rare felines can be seen at Rescate, a rescue center in the rainforest heart of Costa Rica.

In 1989, founder Dennis Janik bought the place as it was more or less in the process of being declared a condemned zoo. Speaking primly about its history, Rescate writes on its website that the zoo was "not a good home for animals." In fact, Janik bought it with the intention of shutting it down. Then he realized most of the animals living there didn't actually have anywhere else to go that wouldn't result in certain death or likely continued exploitation. So Janik changed the mission from destruction to revival. The organization moved down the street to give the animals some much-needed room, changed its legal name, and transformed itself into the only wildlife hospital in Costa Rica. Today, Rescate cares for over 3000 wild animals per year.

Rescate also operates two private centers: one is an 1800-acre (728-hectare) site in the Bosque Escondido Wildlife Refuge on the Nicoya Peninsula and the other is a 90-acre (36-hectare) site in Golfito on the Osa Peninsula. Dedicated staff live at these sites carrying out soft-release processes of endangered animals, ensuring they have the best chance of survival.

LOCATION

Alajuela, Costa Rica.

La Garita de Alajuela is a 15-minute drive from Juan Santamaría International Airport and a 40-minute drive from San José. If you are coming by taxi or local bus, your driver may better recognize the old name, "Rescate Animal Zooave."

SPECIAL NOTES

The center is open 9am-5pm, 365 days a year. (Imagine having a jaguar at Christmas! But then not having to worry about taking care of it because it's living its best life in a Central American jungle!)

If you don't want to just visit but want to live here, they have a wildlife veterinary internship program.

The mission of Rescate is firmly focused on rehabilitation and release. However, that is not always possible, in which case, the animal becomes part of Rescate's Lifetime Care Sanctuary. This is where humans like us can pay to (politely) ooh and aww at them.

There are three sections of the center, but the Sanctuary is the only one open to the public. Visitors walk along a 1.5-mile (2.4km) stone walkway framed by verdant flowers and every shade of green leaf that can climb out of a tropical forest. The route takes you past the edges of the enclosures of the 125 species of animals who live here full-time. Some of the energetic presence of the zoo still remains: there are photo frames where kids can cuddle stuffed sloths, as well as colorful restaurants.

Self-tours through the sanctuary are available, but for a better shot at seeing the animals, go with a guided tour. It's a thorough 2½ hours and runs twice daily. The guides at Rescate know and love these animals; they are experts at pointing out a camouflaged body cleverly tucked away into dark emerald bushes, or spotting in which patch of forked sunlight a gleaming eye can be caught watching you. The prices of the guided tours are kept deliberately low in a lovely act of human generosity.

If you happen to be a bird person in addition to a cat person, Rescate was basically built for you. About 100 exotic, rare Central American birds live here, flitting, singing and flapping to their hearts' content. There is also a wide variety of reptiles, from pythons and boas to tortoises and box turtles. In fact, most of the animals here aren't actually cats. But if you are looking to see the cats of Central America in their natural environment, and support a center doing the real legwork of conservation and education about Central American biodiversity, this is definitely your place.

Sixto, a jaguar, at Rescate.

Turpentine Creek Wildlife Rescue

LOCATION
Arkansas, USA

239 Turpentine Creek Lane, Eureka Springs.

Have you ever started taking care of a stray cat in your neighborhood, only to have people start bringing you more and more, until suddenly you're the neighbor with cat treats in every pocket?

That's more or less how Turpentine Creek Wildlife Rescue started. In 1978, a zoo employee and his family wound up with a tiger that a friend of theirs received as payment for a debt. Unable to turn their backs on animals in need, the Jackson family gained a reputation as a safe place for animals that were rapidly outgrowing the sketchy situations they were trafficked into. And although Turpentine Creek Wildlife Rescue is focused on big cats (and a handful of bears), it feels weird not to mention the Netflix-shaped elephant in the room. Even if you didn't see it, you probably heard about *Tiger King*, the viral documentary series about the US's relationship with big cats and people who exploit animals. And if that's your only impression of big cat rescues, I wouldn't blame you if you associated them solely with cartoonish villainy.

Good news: Turpentine Creek Wildlife Rescue is the actual safe haven you hoped those other places would be.

They're a GFAS-recognized nonprofit, a member of the BCSA, and have rescued over 500 animals (some of whom were relocated from other facilities that may or may not have been featured on TV). All tours are guided, and access to older or more sensitive animals is limited to protect their well-being.

Places like Turpentine Creek are ensuring these animals can live out their lives in peace and dignity, while working hard to make America's big cat trade a thing of the past.

Plus, if you've ever wanted to fall asleep to the sound of lions singing the song of their people, you can actually spend the night here. In addition to regular day passes, Turpentine Creek has lodging available, ranging from decked-out tents to fully furnished cabins (complete with a fire pit and hot tub). If you'd prefer to provide your own accommodations, RV parking and campsites are available on the property.

SPECIAL NOTES

Visiting hours are 8:30am-4pm daily (hours vary on holidays). Admission varies depending on your tour package, but basic day passes (entry plus a 1-hour tram tour) are $35 ($32 online) for adults and $25 ($22 online) for military veterans and children 12 and under.

If you want to take an extended tour, they ask that you book in advance: turpentinecreek.org.

Dillian, a bobcat who's nearly 20 years old.

Wild Cat Conservation Centre

It's a hard truth that cats have gained a bad rap in Australia (and in New Zealand). There are no native felines here. English colonizers brought the first *Felis catus* over on ships and let them loose into the blazing continent, assuming they would help control pests, just as they had done back home. Instead, it was the cats themselves that became the pests. That characterization might offend some readers, but with the killing of 1.5 billion birds per year and the extinction of 22 species of mammals, it is hard not to understand how the locals came to see cats as not much else than pint-sized, furry murder machines. Multiple programs have been enacted to return the ecosystem to normal, with some success, including the encouragement of indoor adoptions. Today, about 40% of Australians and Kiwis have a beloved pet cat, but the feline reputation at large has never seemed to fully recover. Feral cats, while existing in large numbers, are not exactly celebrated as community cats in Australia.

Numerous charity groups provide effective and ethical population control through TNR, healthcare, and adoptions for strays. But if you're coming Down Under to cheat on your cat at home, your best bet is to go for exotics. Tiny ones. This is who's hanging out at the Wild Cat Conservation Centre, an hour northwest of Sydney.

Most wildcat sanctuaries focus on big cat royalty like lions and tigers, but the founder of Australia's only felid sanctuary wanted to change that. Ben Britton saw that 99% of international conservation funding was directed

LOCATION
New South Wales, Australia.

Your best bet is to drive the 40 miles (65km) from Sydney to Wilberforce. The exact address of the Centre is given after booking a tour.

SPECIAL NOTES

Personalized, private tours run about AUS$280-420 (US$200-300) for up to six people. While you can walk in the Centre's savanna with the wild cats, touching them is strictly prohibited, and photos are not permitted (although the staff will do their best to catch you and a cat in the same shot). Check out the latest schedule at wildcatcentre.org.au.

toward saving the seven largest species of cats. Meanwhile, there were 33 different (dare we say "fun-sized") wildcats in great need of support, but rarely getting any attention. Thus, the Wild Cat Conservation Centre was born, just outside the historic pioneer town of Wilberforce in New South Wales. You can find a number of cheetahs here roaming Australia's answer to the African savanna. But the Centre's real work is on endangered exotics that you are far less likely to have heard of, such as caracals, clouded leopards, fishing cats and servals.

The Centre has a carefully conducted breeding program, supporting the birth of endangered cats in order to return them to the wild. Cubs born at the centre live with their mothers and begin their rewilding journey, eventually making their way across the ocean to be released into their native homeland. Unlike some rescue centers, the human staff here are not hands-off; many often get quite chummy with their long-term, older charges that are not being rewilded. Seeing a cheetah kitten happily lick the face of a khaki-clad wildlife veterinarian can feel counter-intuitive to the ethos of "hands-off rehabilitation." However, these are humans and animals that have had an opportunity to build an authentic, care-based relationship. You, an outsider, won't get to play butterfly kisses with a baby cheetah here, but the Centre does offer private tours. Limited groups of adults can enter and watch the cats hop, prowl, bolt and play in the closest thing you can get to their native habitat outside of Africa.

A clouded leopard seen on a twilight tour at the Wildcat Conversation Centre in Australia.

BIG CATS

PUBLIC PARKS

Big Cats: Public Parks

WE CAN THINK OF no better way to see a big cat than in its natural habitat.

Cats roam more or less wherever they want – must be nice to be an apex predator – and nature doesn't see man-made borders. That being said, there are specific lines humans have carved onto the map for the benefit of animals as much as ourselves – gigantic territories where big cats can go about their regular routines, and humans can respectfully lose their minds watching them do it.

These public parks are protected from industrialization and development, nurturing ecosystems with dazzling arrays of flora and fauna. The cats are often at the top of the food chain, but there is just as much to see below. That's the beauty of a natural habitat.

We don't recommend specific tour companies, but we encourage you to select one with a focus on ethics and respectful treatment of animals. This means no chasing, shouting, disturbing or otherwise interfering with their natural behaviors.

If you decide to skip a tour company and go alone, that advice still applies. Not just for the sake of the cats. Consider that you are well-marbled and would pair well with a side of hyena.

Masai Mara National Reserve

LOCATION
Southwestern Kenya.

The most popular road entry is Sekenani Gate, about 143 miles (230km) from Nairobi. If you book with a safari, the trip will start from your lodge.

Masai Mara is one of Earth's most unique and ecologically rich environments. Visiting it firsthand feels a bit like staring at the stars on a clear night – awe-inspiring in its beauty, but also accompanied by a vague sense of danger. It reminds you both of how powerless you are as an individual, but also how interconnected all life is; each living being is but a single stitch in an infinite tapestry of indescribable beauty and complexity.

But *this* part of the tapestry has cats. Big, dangerous cats.

If you're drawn to educational cat content, you've probably seen the Masai Mara National Reserve mentioned by name in *Big Cat Diary*, or any of a number of other nature documentaries. This is one of the most reliable places on Earth to scope out big cats in their natural habitat, going through their daily routines: hunting, drinking, nursing, sleeping, and whatever passes for the lion equivalent of arguing with your spouse about who should clean up dinner.

If your early childhood love of cats was partially formed by *The Lion King*, you might find yourself feeling as though you've seen the Masai Mara before – at least a version of it. The film was a visual love letter to the neighboring wonderlands of the Serengeti and the Masai Mara.

The reserve is home to a staggering number of noteworthy animals, including lions, cheetahs, leopards, and also wildebeests, rhinos, zebras, giraffes, elephants and hippos. It was founded in part to encourage and preserve Africa's Great Migration event – a parade of animals so spectacular,

it frequently lands the Masai Mara on lists tabulating the modern Wonders of the World.

There are plenty of companies that offer tours and accommodations through the park, ranging from basic to luxury packages. Most people visit via a guided safari. Although you can technically go in on your own, this is strongly discouraged by the park personnel, who will have to respond to your distress call if you're stuck in the mud while being slowly surrounded by a pride of female lions – assuming they even get your distress call.

It's generally best not to interact with wild animals, so avoid any company that promises to let you. The idea here is that you get to see these majestic predators in their most authentic habitats. This is best done through binoculars, or in close silence. You want to see them, not bother them. It's recommended to plan ahead, create a short list of tour packages you like, send inquiries to two or three safaris, and wait to hear back. The Maasai people, who are indigenous to Masai Mara Reserve, lead a handful of safari programs, which are rumored to be some of the best.

SPECIAL NOTES

Masai Mara is linked with Serengeti National Park in Tanzania; many safari companies offer a seamless transition between the parks, so you can follow the animals more organically.

A budget safari (for about 4 days) can cost as little as $600-$800.

A private luxury safari (7 days) can be as much as $4,700-$6,100 or more.

BEST TIME TO VISIT

Generally, the best time of year for weather and animal sightings is June-October, particularly from August-October if you're interested in catching the northern leg of the Great Migration.

The best way to see cheetahs is in their natural habitat--and from a distance.

Pench Tiger Reserve

At the heart of India is a jungle – tall spines of teak trees cutting through golden mist, birdsong radiating from a leafy canopy, and fuzzy-headed langurs hopping and hooting from the ground bushes. And just there in the tall grass – a pair of glowing yellow eyes, watching you from across the forest.

There are a healthy handful of tiger sanctuaries in central India, but the leader has to be Pench Tiger Reserve. The park straddles two states (Madhya Pradesh and Maharashtra), and is also the fabled forest that inspired Rudyard Kipling's *The Jungle Book*. Fun fact though: the Englishman never actually set foot in the Pench jungle; he wrote his timeless classic based on the accounts and descriptions of other parts of India. So, if you visit Pench and wonder why it doesn't totally match up to the place you read about as a kid – it's not you, it's Kipling.

Pench is the throne room of the Bengal tiger, but also contains scores of Indian leopards, and even the occasional cheetah. Naturalists attribute the park's large number of big cats to its vast biodiversity, which includes upward of 300 bird species, sloth bears, wild boar, foxes, hyenas, langur monkeys, deer, antelope, Indian bison and much, much more. In other words, you're basically entering a Michelin-star buffet of big cat prey. The park, however, wants to make sure you remain at your present rung of the food chain, which is why no one is allowed in without a guide.

Single-day safaris are the primary way humans hang out in Pench. Visitors can buy a seat on an open-air bus, or rent a private Jeep with a guide.

LOCATION

Central India.

Fly or take a train to Nagpur, then catch a bus to travel the 98km (60 miles) to Pench. The park is ringed by multiple "gates." Turia Gate, on the southern side of the park, is the closest to the Tiger Reserve.

SPECIAL NOTES

A number of hotels and guesthouses ring the park.

You can rent a private Jeep or grab a seat on a shared one. Ticket prices can fluctuate, and foreigners may be charged a higher ticket price than Indian nationals. You can buy tickets at the park directly, at forest.mponline.gov.in (with a valid Indian mobile number), or your guesthouse can help you.

Walk-up tickets are typically available every day on a first-come, first-served basis, or you can book ahead on the park's government website. Safaris take off in the morning, afternoon, or, for the especially adventurous, at night.

Multiday safari operators are also at the ready. These are premium (and pricey) affairs, complete with morning chai among Arjuna trees, plush canopy beds in glamping huts on the edges of the park, and a wise, protective guide who can tell you when to look up to spot the leopard snoozing on a tree bough right above your head. The only thing you need is a pair of binoculars. Guided group backpacking trips and cycling tours are also available from private tour companies.

Only 2500 Bengal tigers remain in the wild, though this is an increase from previous decades, thanks in huge part to conservation efforts by global organizations like WWF, Pench Tiger Reserve, and its associated friends. It's quite rare to see a Bengal tiger in their natural habitat, so if that vision is on your bucket list, this is the place.

Pench National Park is usually open from October to June, but is often closed between July and September due to monsoon floods. Summer (March to June) is hot and busy, but also the most likely time to spot big cats as they gather at watering holes to cool off.

Wear neutral clothing in the park, as bright colors tend to deter animals.

A female leopard perches on a tree at the Pench Tiger Reserve in India.

The Luangwa Valley

LOCATION
Zambia.

Mfuwe is the main town and regional airport. From there, your safari company or hotel can arrange a shuttle directly to the park entrance.

The Luangwa Valley is home to both North Luangwa and South Luangwa National Parks. North Luangwa is the wilder of the two, with almost no roads, hotels, or tourist infrastructure. As annoying as overtourism is, this isn't necessarily a good thing, if you value your life. Every year, at least a few souls are claimed by crocodiles, elephants and/or lions within North Luangwa. So, do what you want, but don't say nobody warned you.

South Luangwa is the more tourist-friendly of the two parks, with a few small-scale, high quality lodges – but the animals are still firmly charge. This is the kind of place where a pride of lions, having sized you up and surmised that you aren't much of a threat, might use your safari car as a hiding spot while they scope out some wildebeest, or a family of elephants might wander into your hotel's lobby in search of a loose mango.

South Luangwa began its life in 1904 as a place where English colonists would come to prove how masculine they were by shooting animals between tea breaks. Then along came Norman Carr, who wondered, "Could one train Europeans to enjoy animals while they were still alive?" In 1950, Carr petitioned Nsefu, Paramount Chief of the local Kunda people, to set aside a portion of their land as a game reserve. The Europeans responded well, apparently quite interested in shooting the animals with cameras instead of guns. Proceeds from the tours went back into the local community, and ecotourism in Africa was born.

Lion sightings are common in South Luangwa, along with lagoons teeming with crocodiles and hippos, parades of elephants, herds of zebras, gangs of laughing hyenas, and colorful clouds of birds. The Luangwa River defines the park, flooding the grasslands into emerald fields during the wet season, and then receding back into itself, allowing the woodlands to ripen into dry gold. When the river is low, uneasy truces are forged between prey and predator, as every animal must approach the same riverbanks for a drink. Humans, gaping from safari cars, are in for a treat.

South Luangwa is considered by many to be the best game park in Africa, while also being less crowded than the Masai Mara or the Serengeti. All lodges surrounding the park organize safari drives or walks, either single or multiday. These safaris are led by a Zambian guide armed with a wealth of knowledge and a very large gun. Night safaris are an especially cherished time to glimpse a leopard dragging a midnight impala snack up into a tree.

You can also drive yourself into South Luangwa, and do away with a guide entirely. Keep in mind, walking alone into the bush is technically forbidden. The naturalists that work here have some of the most difficult jobs in the world. They are extremely self-sufficient, going on 10-day trips into about 2.2 million acres (890,000 hectares) of apex predator wilderness to track migrations and arrest poachers. You are the least of their problems. Just understand that if you go it alone, something far toothier than a human might catch you.

BEST TIME TO VISIT

October, before the rains start and the river swells, is considered the best time to visit. However, the heat can be extreme, so take appropriate precautions.

SPECIAL NOTES

Foreign visitors can expect to pay $20-30 per day as an entry fee into South Luangwa. If you're staying at a bush camp within the park, you don't have to worry about paying this every day.

South Luangwa is less busy than other African wilderness parks, but that's largely due to limited accommodations than lack of interest. Availability during the open season can be competitive, so booking in advance is recommended.

A big leopard has a big yawn in the South Luangwa National Park in Zambia.

Serengeti National Park

Of all the epic parks within Africa, the king is, arguably, the Serengeti. It is one of Earth's few terrains that has barely changed over the course of a million years. Fossils unearthed here help humans trace the story of our evolution from four-footed hominid to bipedal genius. A galactic number of zebras, antelopes, wildebeest and gazelles band together each year to march 500 miles (805km), in a phenomenon aptly dubbed the Great Migration. The hot, windy sky stretches out in sunset flames virtually every night, punctuated by slabs of alien rock and the levitating branches of acacia trees. In the distance, there are cats upon cats: cheetahs dash, leopards perch, servals prowl, and the largest lion population on Earth roars its hellos.

A complete list of wildlife viewable in the Serengeti could fill an entire book (in fact, many authors have tried). There is everything here from elephants to hippos, giraffes to crocodiles, and a never-ending array of birds – some appear to have flown straight off a 1990s Lisa Frank poster, while others, like the crowned eagle, are so large, they hunt monkeys.

Due to its immense fame (many of the landscapes here were the inspirational backdrop for *The Lion King)*, tourist infrastructure is some of the easiest to find, and also some of the poshest. The park got its start as a game reserve in 1930 thanks to Richard Hingston, who sought to ensure that the temptations of economic development (notably, from his own colonial government) did not destroy it. Others opposed the park's creation, as it would push out the indigenous people – that is, the people who had been living on the land

LOCATION
Tanzania

Most people opt to fly into Kilimanjaro International Airport then take a taxi or shuttle to Arusha, the main starting point for most safaris. The airport in Arusha caters mostly to private flights.

SPECIAL NOTES

The Ndutu area in the south, which borders the Ngorongoro Conservation Area, is known for its high concentration of big cats.

The Serengeti is bordered by several other conservation areas. Humans see the lines, but the animals don't. If you have experienced sticker shock at the cost of an organized Serengeti tour, consider looking into bordering parks, which have similar wildlife opportunities, including walking safaris, at slightly less apex prices.

harmoniously for generations – in the name of "conservation." However, today, a tenuous peace seems to have been struck between all humans involved, with the deeper understanding that everyone wants this place to stick around for a very long time.

The default way of entering Serengeti National Park is through a licensed safari operator. These come in a wide variety of flavors, from aristocratic luxury to rugged camping. With either choice, buckle up before you check the price tags, which typically start at $3000. However, all come with an armed guide who is usually chatting with other guides, gently ushering you to witness the most action. You can also enter the park without a guide – renting your own Jeep, planning your own route, and paying fees directly to the park and the lodges.

What is likely to be on your premium-priced safari menu is lions upon lions upon lions – sunbathing on rocky outcrops in the heat of the day, pouncing in play, or perhaps, if you're lucky (or unlucky), on the hunt. Lions in the Serengeti are at the top of the food chain, which can mean some disturbing sights. However, Serengeti cats have seen safari Jeeps their entire life, and tend to be quite comfortable around them. They may even wander alongside yours for a while. Keeping up with a 100mph (161km/h) cheetah may be out of your reach in a Jeep on a dirt road, but you can still expect to see some, zooming in the distance, in a busy hunt for dinner.

BEST TIMES TO VISIT

The dry seasons, from June-August and December-February, are considered the best times to visit. These months offer a lower chance of tires stuck in the mud and better opportunities to see animals gathered at watering holes. Late summer is the most crowded, when the Great Migration is in full swing, and the cats, not far behind, are on the hunt. However, June is considered the best time to visit by many in the know: it precedes the peak crowds of August while animals gear up in the south for their migration north.

Something in the distance has the attention of a lion and his cub in Serengeti National Park.

Parque Nacional Pumalín & Parque Nacional Patagonia

LOCATION

Southern Chile.

These new Chilean parks define the word "remote." Getting to either Parque Nacional Pumalín or Parque Nacional Patagonia will require renting a private plane, or the patience for a very long drive.

When you dream about a hiking trip in Patagonia, the first images that come to mind are probably from Torres del Paine: the surreal backpacker's playground dotted with stone towers and snow-laced glacier lakes. Mountain lions positively thrive there, and it is remarked as an excellent place for puma tracking. But good luck ever actually seeing one of them with your own eyes. Torres del Paine is as crowded as it is gorgeous, and mountain lions, master introverts that they are, are not likely to be caught hanging out next to a hundred international tourists who are forced to share one campground and four toilets.

A lot of people agreed that there needed to be more national parks in southern Chile – quieter ones. In the mid-1990s, Doug Tompkins, founder of The North Face, quit his job to move here with his wife, Kris Tompkins, former CEO of the Patagonia clothing company. The two were on a mission to dedicate the rest of their lives (and fortune) to buying up neglected ranch land and mines in the hinterlands of southern Chile. Doug's goal was to buy it, revive the native flora and fauna, and donate it back to the Chilean government in the form of national parks.

Many Chileans raised an eyebrow at the mad Americans who were snatching up millions of acres of their backcountry on a nebulous promise to

do good. But in 2018, Chilean president Michelle Bachelet announced that yes, the government would accept one million acres (405,000 hectares) from Tompkins Conservation to create five new national parks and expand three more: 11 million acres (4.5 million hectares) total. It was the largest private land donation in history.

From this, two new national parks were born in Chile: Parque Nacional Pumalín and Parque Nacional Patagonia.

If you're the kind of person whose idea of a dream vacation is having no one around while you prowl through virgin temperate rainforest and reconstituted sub-Antarctic tundra, say hello to paradise. Amenities are slim in both of these infant parks. That is to say, competition for backcountry camping permits is nonexistent. And the mountain lions roam freely, unhampered by noise and hordes of tourists. Rewilding Chile has been at the forefront of species reintroduction and habitat restoration, with a special focus on the nationally symbolic, perilously endangered huemul deer (which the mountain lions also like to eat). Together with the conservation organization Panthera, they have been tracking a steady rise in mountain lions in both parks. Pumalín is seeing a small but encouragingly rising number of mountain lions sneaking through its rainforests. Parque National Patagonia is slightly more reliable for sightings along its spired peaks and stark, windswept plains.

If you don't like the idea of sleeping outside, alone, in the dark, in the middle of nowhere, during your attempt to see an apex predator in the wild, both parks do have (one) lodge. Explora Lodge in Parque Nacional Patagonia offers full- and half-day tours for kayaking, hiking, and puma-watching. Caleta Gonzalo in Pumalín has little rustic cabins set on the fjords.

SPECIAL NOTES

According to one visitor, the pumas never attack humans as they are too busy stuffing themselves with *guanaco*. But we still recommend watching your back if you're going out into these remote parks without a guide.

Kris Tompkins gives the occasional private hiking tour in Parque Nacional Pumalín, if you want to thank her in person.

A puma scans its surroundings in Patagonia.

Resources & Credits

MORE CAT-SPOTTING RESOURCES

The Neighbor's Cat
(theneighborscat.com/blog)
Lists cat cafes by country, active as of 2022

Traveling Cats
(traveling-cats.com)
Detailed reviews and tips for visiting cat-centric locales around the globe

Travel Cat
(yourcatbackpack.com)
A guide to cat-related sites in the world, listed by continent and country, including a custom interactive Google Map

Catlas Obscura
(atlasobscura.com/users/baycurious/lists/catlas-obscura)
"The Cat Lady's Bucket List" of cat colonies and obscure cat iconography

Cat Cafe Map
(catcafemap.com)
An interactive map of all the cat cafes in the world

Cat Photo Safari
(catphotosafari.com)
Photo blog of cats around the world, including tips on where to say hi yourself

Big Cat Sanctuary Alliance
(bigcatalliance.org)
Sanctuary network for the ethical care of big cats

Global Federation of Animal Sanctuaries
(sanctuaryfederation.org)
Globally recognized organization providing standards for legitimate animal sanctuaries (including big cats)

Street Cats and Where to Find Them by Jeff Bogle
(Running Press; 2025)
Photographic memoir of Bogle's cat connections around the world, with helpful tips for future visitors

2: Mika Volkmann/Getty Images; **3:** Mark Carrel/Shutterstock (and repeated throughout the book); **5(t):** Boris15/Shutterstock; **5(bl):** neftali/Shutterstock; **5(br):** Amateur007/Shutterstock; **7:** Wirestock Creators/Shutterstock; **8(t):** Amateur007/Shutterstock; **8(b):** Amateur007/Shutterstock; **9(t):** Amateur007/Shutterstock; **9(b):** Amateur007/Shutterstock; **11:** Tuchong/Imaginechina Limited/Alamy; **12(ctr):** Mika Volkmann/Getty Images; **12(bkgd):** Page Light Studios/Shutterstock; **14:** Boris15/Shutterstock; **15(ctr):** Alex_Mastro/Shutterstock; **15(bkgd):** Viacheslav Lopatin/Shutterstock; **16(ctr):** Riccardo Milani/Redux; **16(bkgd:** NurPhoto/Getty Images; **17:** Boris15/Shutterstock; **19:** FlowerGirl5/Shutterstock; **20:** Lefteris Papaulakis/Shutterstock; **21(ctr):** Courtesy of Le Café des Chats; **21(bkgd):** Courtesy of Le Café des Chats; **22(ctr):** FooTToo/Shutterstock; **22(bkgd):** Matt Munro for Lonely Planet; **24:** Brendan Howard/Shutterstock; **25(ctr):** Anastasia Bielokon/Shutterstock; **25(bkgd):** jacky chapman/Alamy; **26(ctr):** Matthias Scholz/Alamy; **26(bkgd):** Martin M303/Shutterstock; **27:** ilapinto/Shutterstock; **28:** Simone Padovani/Shutterstock; **30:** YANGCHAO/Shutterstock; **31(ctr):** Marco Serena Photographer/Alamy; **31(bkgd):** Joaolpascoa_Photography/Shutterstock; **32(ctr):** Heather Schor/Shutterstock; **32(bkgd):** Anthem Video for Lonely Planet; **34:** spatuletail/Shutterstock; **35(ctr):** Nate Smallwood; **35(bkgd):** Nate Smallwood; **36(ctr):** Nate Smallwood; **36(bkgd):** Nate Smallwood; **37:** H M Thompson/Shutterstock; **39:** Nate Smallwood; **40:** Roberto Lusso/Shutterstock; **41(ctr):** Courtesy of Pittsburgh Prison Cats; **41(bkgd):** Courtesy of Roman Hladio and NEXTpittsburgh; **42(ctr):** Duygu_11/Shutterstock; **42(bkgd):** Mark Read for Lonely Planet; **44:** rook76/Shutterstock; **45(ctr):** Emre Boz/Shutterstock; **45(bkgd):** Emre Boz/Shutterstock; **46(ctr):** Natalia Kirsanova/Shutterstock; **46(bkgd):** Ayhan Altun/Getty Images; **47:** Amateur007/Shutterstock; **49:** vhpicstock/Shutterstock; **50:** World of Stamps/Shutterstock; **51(ctr):** Lizavetta/Shutterstock; **51(bkgd):** MILA PARH/Shutterstock; **52(ctr):** Tuul & Bruno Morandi/Getty Images; **52(bkgd):** Lottie Davies for Lonely Planet; **54:** slexp880/Shutterstock; **55(ctr):** Aflo Co. Ltd./Alamy; **55(bkgd):** Hannari_eli/Shutterstock; **56(ctr):** PJ_Photography/Shutterstock; **56(bkgd):** Piyawan Charoenlimkul/Shutterstock; **57:** Nicescene/Shutterstock; **59:** Stephane BDC/Shutterstock; **60:** Jonathan Stokes for Lonely Planet; **62:** slexp880/Shutterstock; **63(ctr):** Elli Hannari; **63(bkgd):** Carol Di Rienzo Cornwell/Alamy; **64(ctr):** freedom-man3/Shutterstock; **64(bkgd):** Sanga Park /Shutterstock; **66:** Lefteris Papaulakis/Shutterstock; **67(ctr):** MartiBstock/Shutterstock; **67(bkgd):** YAMASA/Shutterstock; **68(ctr):** Courtesy of Kitten Coffee Garden, Taipai; **68(bkgd):** Courtesy of Kitten Coffee Garden, Taipai; **69:** Amateur007/Shutterstock; **71:** Tree suriyakul/Shutterstock; **72:** neftali/Shutterstock; **73(ctr):** Noy47/Shutterstock; **73(bkgd):** Nowaczyk/Shutterstock; **74(ctr):** Nakaharu Line/Unsplash; **74(bkgd):** DuKai photographer/Getty Images; **76:** neftali/Shutterstock; **77(ctr):** AFP/Getty Images; **77(bkgd):** Yuen Man Cheung /Alamy; **78(ctr):** Nyoto/Shutterstock; **78(bkgd):** itsskin/Getty Images; **79:** StampCollection/Alamy; **80:** Christian J Kober/Alamy; **82:** Joinmepic/Shutterstock; **83(ctr):** woodvillage/Shutterstock; **83(bkgd):** Xinhua/Alamy; **84(ctr):** Anastasia Sotchenko/Shutterstock; **84(bkgd):** Marco Argüello for Lonely Planet; **87:** Majna/Shutterstock; **88:** Amateur007/Shutterstock; **89(ctr):** Dragica Nikolovska/Shutterstock; **89(bkgd):** Marco Argüello for Lonely Planet; **90(ctr):** Kirk Fisher/Shutterstock; **90(bkgd):** Jaione_Garcia/Shutterstock; **91:** Lestertair/Shutterstock; **92:** Markus Gebauer/Shutterstock; **94:** World of Stamps/Shutterstock; **95(ctr):** vangelispidiakis; **95(bkgd):**vangelispidiakis; **96(ctr):**valerii eidlin/Shutterstock; **96(bkgd):** Sivan Askayo for Lonely Planet; **99:** Ross Robinson/Alamy; **100:** Amateur007/Shutterstock; **101(ctr):** Jose Perez/Bauer-Griffin/Getty Images; **101(bkgd):** Simone Pitrolo/Shutterstock; **102(ctr):** Courtesy of The Algonquin Hotel; **102(bkgd):** Alex_Mastro/Shutterstock; **103:** Boris15/Shutterstock; **104:** Neilson Abeel Jr/Alamy; **106:** aniejasin/Shutterstock; **107(ctr):** Zhen qin/Courtesy of The Cat Museum of New York City; **107(bkgd):** Zhen Qin/Courtesy of The Cat Museum of New York City; **108(ctr):** stefanophotographer/Shutterstock; **108(bkgd):** Peter Seaward for Lonely Planet; **111:** Alina Prokudina/Shutterstock; **112:** Boris15/Shutterstock; **113(ctr):** Thisun Piyasena/Alamy; **113(bkgd):** Halit Sadik/Shutterstock; **114(ctr):** Eman Kazemi/Alamy; **114(bkgd):** Orhan Cam/Shutterstock; **115:** Boris15/Shutterstock; **117:** naTsumi/Shutterstock; **118:** rook76/Shutterstock; **119(ctr):** Sherif M. Alyamany/Shutterstock; **119(bkgd):** Mike P Shepherd/Alamy; **121:** MarinaNov/Shutterstock; **122(ctr):** Scott Russell/Courtesy of Cat Town; **122(bkgd):** Mark Read for Lonely Planet; **124:** Amateur007/Shutterstock; **125(ctr):** Courtesy of Cat Town; **125(bkgd):**Courtesy of Cat Town; **126(ctr):** Becca Hunt; **126(bkgd):** Becca Hunt; **127:** Amateur007/Shutterstock; **128:** Courtesy of Cat Town; **130:** neftali/Shutterstock; **131(ctr):** Diana Helmuth; **131(bkgd):** Diana Helmuth; **132(ctr):** Tuul and Bruno Morandi/Alamy; **132(bkgd):** Sankei/Getty Images; **134:** spatuletail/Shutterstock; **135(ctr):** Tristan deBrauwere; **135(bkgd):** Tristan deBrauwere; **136(ctr):** Martin Bertrand/Alamy; **136(bkgd):** Alexander Gafarro/Shutterstock; **137:** Sergey Kohl/Shutterstock; **138:** Amateur007/Shutterstock; **139(ctr):** Oleg Doroshenko/Alamy; **139(bkgd):** Julian Love for Lonely Planet; **140:** Kati Lenart/Shutterstock; **143:** negatina/Getty Images; **144(ctr):** Lori Barbely/Alamy; **144(bkgd):** Lori Barbely/Alamy; **145:** Zoltan Katona/Shutterstock; **147:** Courtesy of Lānaʻi Cat Sanctuary; **148:** Courtesy of Lānaʻi Cat Sanctuary; **150:** tristan tan/Shutterstock; **151(ctr):** PhotopankPL /Shutterstock; **151(bkgd):** Herrieynaha/Shutterstock; **152:** Tupungato/Shutterstock; **155:** DreamArchitect/Shutterstock; **156(ctr):** Diego Grandi/Shutterstock; **156(bkgd):** Kirill Neiezhmakov/Shutterstock; **157:** ilapinto/Shutterstock; **159:** Ryan Chin/Shutterstock; **160:** neftali/Shutterstock; **161(ctr):** GAGAnuma/Shutterstock; **161(bkgd):** Leung Cho Pan/Panther Media Global/Alamy; **162:** Here it is/Getty Images; **164:** grassflowerhead/Alamy; **166(ctr):** The Washington Post/Getty Images; **166(bkgd):** YAO DEKANG/Shutterstock; **167:** Reyanaska/Shutterstock; **169:** Joey Huang/Unsplash; **170(ctr):** Courtesy of The Wild Animal Sanctuary; **170(bkgd):** Courtesy of the Wild Cat Conservation Centre; **173:** Stefanie Kraus/Courtesy of WildCat Ridge Sanctuary;**174:** spatuletail/Shutterstock; **175(ctr):** Thoroughly Travel; **175(bkgd):** Al Argueta/Alamy; **176:** Courtesy of ARCAS Wildlife Rescue Center; **178(ctr):** Stefanie Kraus/Courtesy of WildCat Ridge Sanctuary; **178(bkgd):** Stefanie Kraus/Courtesy of WildCat Ridge Sanctuary ; **179:** IgorGolovniov/Shutterstock; **181:** Stefanie Kraus/Courtesy of WildCat Ridge Sanctuary; **182:** Koray Olsen/Shutterstock; **183(ctr):** Christine Humphreys/The Wild Animal Sanctuary; **183(bkgd):** RJ Sangosti/Getty Images; **184:** Courtesy of the Wild Animal Sanctuary; **186(ctr):** Photographer and Biologist: Eduardo Rodríguez Romano, Rescue Center: Rescate Wildlife Rescue Center, Garita, Alajuela; **186(bkgd):** Jonathan Gregson for Lonely Planet; **187:** Boris15/Shutterstock; **189:** Photographer and Biologist: Eduardo Rodríguez Romano Rescue Center: Rescate Wildlife Rescue Center, Garita, Alajuela; **190:** spatuletail/Shutterstock; **191(ctr):** Courtesy of Turpentine Creek Wildlife Refuge; **191(bkgd):** Kansas City Star/Getty Images; **192:** Courtesy of Turpentine Creek Wildlife Refuge; **194(ctr):** Courtesy of Wild Cat Conservation Centre, Australia; **194(bkgd):** Courtesy of Wild Cat Conservation Centre; **195:** Tony Smith/Alamy; **197:** Courtesy of Wild Cat Conservation Centre, Australia; **198(ctr):** Foto 4440/Shutterstock; **198(bkgd):** Anup Shah/Getty Images; **200:** Boris15/Shutterstock; **201(ctr):** Budimir Jevtic/Shutterstock; **201(bkgd):** Bearfoot Contessa/Shutterstock; **202:** Nitin Vyas/500px/Getty Images; **204(ctr):** Manuel ROMARIS/Getty Images; **204(bkgd):** Venturing wild/Shutterstock; **205:** rook76/Shutterstock; **207:** Sourabh Bharti/Alamy; **208:** Al.geba/Shutterstock; **209(ctr):** WilcoUK/Shutterstock; **209(bkgd):** sherly348/500px/Getty Images; **210:** Marco Pozzi Photographer/Getty Images; **212(ctr):** Judging_Jester/Shutterstock; **212(bkgd):** Joel Shawn/Shutterstock; **213:** neftali/Shutterstock; **215:** Hawatrending/Shutterstock; **216:** tristan tan/Shutterstock; **217(ctr):** Wirestock Creators/Shutterstock; **217(bkgd):** Naeemphotographer2/Shutterstock; **218:** Ralph Lee Hopkins/SuperStock/Alamy; **220:** Katho Menden/Shutterstock; **224:** Daniel Dorsa for Lonely Planet.

Index

Where to Cheat on Your Cat
November 2026
Published by Lonely Planet Global Limited
CRN: 554153
ISBN: 978 1 83758 697 4

10 9 8 7 6 5 4 3 2 1
Printed in Malaysia

Publishing Director: Piers Pickard
Publisher: Becca Hunt
Editors: Becca Hunt, Joanna Cooke, Molly Glover
Creative Direction: Emily Dubin
Design: Taylor Miles Hopkins
Print Production: Nigel Longuet

Stay in Touch
lonelyplanet.com/contact

Lonely Planet Global Limited
Digital Depot, Roe Lane (off Thomas St),
Digital Hub, Dublin 8,
D08 TCV4
Ireland
(EU authorised representative)

FSC™ www.fsc.org MIX Paper | Supporting responsible forestry FSC™ C021741

Paper in this book is certified against the Forest Stewardship Council™ standards. FSC™ promotes environmentally responsible, socially beneficial and economically viable management of the world's forests.

1984
GATOS
forever usa
adopt a shel
भारत INDIA
25
जिम कार्बेट शताब्दी
1875-1955
JIM CORBETT CENTENARY
GUYANA
$ 2
AMERICAN SHORTHAIRED
1987
中華民國郵票 REPUBLIC OF CHINA
TÜRKIYE CUMHURIYETI
posta
100
kuruş
Ankara kedisi
Posta Română
10
BANI
60
BANI
Posta Română
PANTHERA UNCIA
1994
20
КЫРГЫЗСТАН
30
TANZANIA
Maine's cat
200/.
1992
5
1966
30
2,20
中華民國郵票 REPUBLIC OF CHINA
1984
Carapacho-tortuga blanco
CORREOS
P5.00
84
NIPPON